I0762692

SURREALISM
FROM
PARIS TO
SHANGHAI

SURREALISM FROM PARIS TO SHANGHAI

Lauren Walden

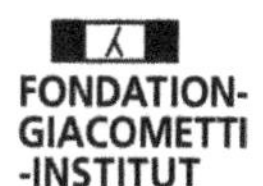

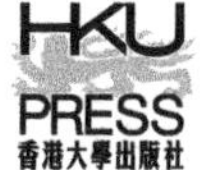

Hong Kong University Press
The University of Hong Kong
Pok Fu Lam Road
Hong Kong
https://hkupress.hku.hk

ISBN 978-988-8842-91-9 (*Hardback*)

This book was first published in French in 2022 in the book series of the 'École des modernités' research programmes developed by the Fondation Giacometti and co-published with Fage éditions.

Fondation Giacometti: Catherine GRENIER (Director)
Soizic WATTINNE (Deputy Director)
Françoise COHEN (Director)
Hugo DANIEL (Head of the École des modernités, Book's scientific direction)
Salomé DOLINSKI (Book's editorial work)
Émilie BOUCHET-LE MAPPIAN (Book's legal issues)

British Library Cataloguing-in-Publication Data
A catalogue record for this book is available from the British Library.

10 9 8 7 6 5 4 3 2 1

Printed and bound by Hang Tai Printing Co., Ltd. in Hong Kong, China

CONTENTS

ACKNOWLEDGEMENTS

I would like to thank all staff at the Giacometti Foundation, the original publishers of this book in French, for recognising the potential of this manuscript and bringing it to fruition. Particular thanks go to Hugo Daniel in this respect for his faith in a transcultural project led by an Early Career Researcher. I also wish to show appreciation for my mentor, Professor Joshua Jiang, who read a first draft of this work. Further to this, my recognition also goes to Paul French who noticed the potential of this text to resonate with Anglophone and Sinophone audiences, bringing it to the attention of Hong Kong University Press for an English version. As a prolific author, Paul helpfully recommended several expansions to the text for its second edition. My thanks also go to the three anonymous peer reviewers whose critique was equally invaluable. Thank you also to Michael Duckworth of Hong Kong University Press for his prompt editorial expertise and smooth communication. Recognition is also due to other staff members at Hong Kong University Press for all their support. I am also indebted to Judith Lingères who helped source the original iconographic elements of this book. On this note, the Li Ching Foundation were most generous in providing images for Pang Xunqin and Sanyu and responding to numerous queries about these artists. Thank you also to Paul Bevan who provided an image from *Wenyi Huabao*, as well as the daughter of Lang Jingshan, Eve Long, who granted permission to reproduce her father's photographs. Thank you to Jean-Pierre Fouilleul who proofread my translations from Chinese. Finally, I wish to thank all members of my family (Ezekiel, Mum, Dad, Melissa) who have always supported my decision to pursue a rewarding yet often precarious career. I hope they will enjoy my first book!

INTRODUCTION

The term 'Surrealism' was first coined by the French poet Guillaume Apollinaire in 1917 to characterise a ballet entitled *Parade*. Comprising set designs and costumes by Pablo Picasso, dancers metamorphosed into skyscrapers and other ciphers of modernity. This ballet and Apollinaire's nascent musings on Surrealism were typified by 'surprising analogies based on reality'.[1] In 1924, the Surrealist movement itself was founded in Paris by the writer and poet André Breton with a more robust philosophical orientation. Bretonian Surrealism adopted the ideas of both Karl Marx and Sigmund Freud, aligning the politics of revolution with the psychology of dreams. The movement gradually gained a significant international following. Yet, China is not a country habitually associated with Surrealism's worldwide expansion and is generally overshadowed by its neighbour Japan.

Several Japanese artists, including Taro Okamoto, were readily assimilated into Surrealist networks with their paintings on display at the key *International Surrealist Exhibition* (1938) that took place at the Galérie des Beaux-Arts in

1. Willard Bohn, 'From Surrealism to Surrealism: Apollinaire and Breton', *The Journal of Aesthetics and Art Criticism* 36, no. 2 (1977): 201.

Paris which saw the group's contribution to the movement formally acknowledged by their Parisian counterparts.[2] Yet, in a disavowal of the colonialist Mercator projection, the infamous *Surrealist Map of the World* (1929) sized nations in accordance with their perceived cultural prowess, positioning China relatively prominently while Japan was completely omitted (Figure 1).

Moreover, in 1925, Breton spoke of plans to visit China in his 'Lettre aux Voyants' [Letter to the seers] describing a dream. He affirmed: 'It appears that I must go to China around 1931 and run great dangers there for twenty years'.[3] This was a journey that Breton would never empirically make, perhaps owing to his superstitious reasoning surrounding the dreamscape. Rather, Breton asserted he could 'transport myself in thought to China much more easily than elsewhere'.[4] Indeed, art historian Mitter's notion of a 'virtual cosmopolis',[5] comprising contact with different nations through print media as opposed to travel, was thoroughly instrumentalised by Breton and his Surrealist coterie.

2. Okamoto (1911–1996) was a Surrealist studying in Paris at the time. Later conscripted into the Japanese army, he became a prisoner of war in China during the Second Sino-Japanese War. Other prominent Japanese Surrealists include Fukuzawa Ichiro, credited with establishing the movement in Japan. In 1936, Ichiro painted the work *Oxen* in the Japanese-occupied territory of Manchuria in northern China, denouncing the conditions under which Chinese colonial subjects lived.
3. André Breton, *Manifestoes of Surrealism*, trans. Richard Seaver and Helen R. Lane (Ann Arbor: University of Michigan Press, 1974), 201.
4. Breton, *Manifestoes of Surrealism*, 201. Whilst I haven't found definitive proof of Breton's early textual engagement with China, it seems probable based on this statement that he was clearly interested in Chinese thought at this juncture.
5. Keith Moxey and Partha Mitter, 'A "Virtual Cosmopolis": Partha Mitter in Conversation with Keith Moxey', *The Art Bulletin* 95, no. 3 (2013): 381–92.

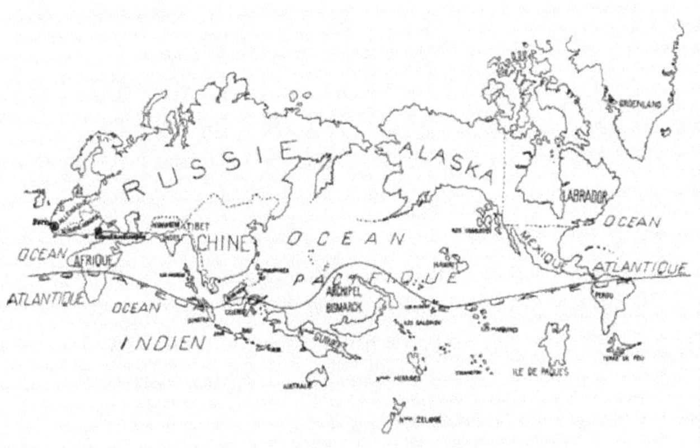

Figure 1. Anon. *The Surrealist Map of the World*, in *Variétés* (Brussels, 1929): 26–27.

Surrealism, although originally conceived in the West, often espoused views that jarred with the rationality of Western civilisation stemming from the enlightenment, a trajectory which was perceived to constrain the imagination. As such, I believe it is valid to question whether Surrealism can be canonised as solely a 'Western' movement while fundamentally opposing its core philosophical trajectory. Hereupon, in 1925, at the very beginning of the Surrealist movement, André Breton comments 'it is as if doors were opening in the Orient, as if the echo of an all-enfolding agitation reached me, as if a breath, which might well be that of Freedom, suddenly makes the old chest of Europe, on which I had gone to sleep, resound'.[6] Hence, the 'Orient' becomes

6. Breton, *Manifestoes of Surrealism*, 201.

synonymous with untrammelled liberty and a capacity for spiritual renewal which Europe can benefit from.

Yet, Surrealism's somewhat idealised, orientalist visions do not preclude engagement with the empirical realities of China during the 1920s and 1930s. Breton also pens another dream in 1926 revolving around 'a city near Shanghai'. This location is couched as the site of an indigenous uprising against colonialism.[7] Indeed, Shanghai had been partially occupied by imperial powers, including France, since the signing of unequal treaties after China's defeat in the First Opium Wars (1839–1842). Shanghai is oneirically reified as a battleground for Surrealism's anti-colonial fervour. Moreover, the Surrealists roundly condemned French colonial enterprise, culminating in the movement's anti-colonial exhibition, mounted in conjunction with the French Communist Party in 1931.

As we shall discover, despite these potent philosophical resonances, the lack of reciprocal involvement between European Surrealists and the Shanghai avant-garde of the 1930s has unfortunately discouraged transnational research in this domain. In fact, Surrealism was highly influential among avant-garde circles in cosmopolitan Shanghai despite their inability to fully penetrate Surrealist spaces in Europe.

7. André Breton, 'Je me trouve en Chine' [I find myself in China]. Bibliothèque Littéraire Jacques Doucet, Paris, Fonds André Breton 02.03.1926: BRT 38.

In particular, the Shanghainese 'Storm Society' [Juelanshe],[8] established by artist Pang Xunqin[9] and artist-critic Ni Yide, specifically credits Surrealism in their founding manifesto of 1932,[10] proclaiming: 'Since the beginning of the 20th century, the European art world has witnessed the advent of new phenomena: the cries of the Fauvists, the deformations of Cubism, the vehemence of Dada and the desires of the Surrealists.'[11] Furthermore, in 1935, a journal called *Yifeng* [Art winds], published a 104-page special edition on Surrealism including a translation of Breton's 1924 *Manifesto* by the Shanghai painter Zhao Shou.[12] This was associated with the Chinese Independent Art Association (1934–1935),[13] whose founders were returning students who had initially encountered Surrealism in Japan. Its founding members were Li Dongping, Liang Xihong, Zhao Shou, Zeng Ming, and French artist André Bessin. Members of this group, such as Zhao Shou and Zeng Ming, formally identified themselves as Surrealists.

Further to these avant-garde groupings which focused on painting, photomontage was also deployed by cartoonists

8. According to the recollections of group member Yang Taiyang: 'We came up with the name [*Storm Society*] together. *Storm Society* expresses the idea of a stormy wave, something very strong and progressive. This stormy wave came from the sea crashing down on this era. A stormy wave, a very powerful one, had been formed.' See 'Yang Taiyang: The Storm Society Interview', in *Shanghai Modern 1914–1945*, ed. Jo-Anne Birnie Danzker, Ken Lum, and Shengtian Zheng (Ostfildern-Ruit: Hatje Cantz, 2004), 242.
9. Pang Xunqin is explored in greater depth in a case study on pp. 24–46.
10. The full manifesto of the Storm Society is reproduced in Appendix I.
11. *Yishu Xunkan* [Art trimonthly] 1, no. 5 (1932): 8.
12. Chinghsin Wu, 'Reality Within and Without: Surrealism in Japan and China in the Early 1930s', *Review of Japanese Culture and Society* 26, no. 1 (2016): 189–208.
13. The Chinese Independent Art Association is explored in a separate chapter on pp. 64–79. The group's name is henceforth abbreviated to CIAA.

in a more political idiom to satirise the semi-colonial cityscape of treaty port Shanghai and serve as a brutal reminder of mounting Japanese aggression. Fine art photography also flourished, artists such as Lang Jingshan utilising experimental Surrealist techniques to embellish the nude female form. While this text focuses on Chinese Surrealism in an art historical context, Surrealist-inspired literature could be found in the work of the new sensationalist writer and essayist Shi Zhecun. According to Chinese literature scholar Rosenmeier, the New Sensationalists 'most famous works reflect, the speed, chaos and intensity of the metropolis . . . they saw themselves as an avant-garde that rejected the tenets of realism and social engagement'.[14] Shi had composed short stories such as *At the Paris Cinema* (1931) and *Demon's Way* (1931), which interrogated Shanghainese contradictions between a cosmopolitan, yet resolutely colonial modernity, enmeshed with explorations of the city's urbanites via Freudian psychoanalysis.

As Chinese Studies scholar Schaefer reveals, Shi turned down an offer by the American Surrealist poet Eugène Jolas to dedicate a special issue of *Xiandai* [Les Contemporains] magazine to Surrealism, believing that it would attract criticism as fantastical escapism, something that had previously been said of his own work.[15] In the text 'Miró's painting', Shi recollects that he had several links with Chinese artists who had studied abroad, several of whom had nevertheless produced front covers for *Xiandai* in a Surrealist style such

14. Christopher Rosenmeier, 'The New Sensationists: Shi Zhecun, Mu Shiying, Liu Na'Ou', in *Routledge Handbook of Modern Chinese Literature*, ed. Ming Dong Gu (Oxford: Routledge, 2018).
15. William Schaefer, *Shadow Modernism: Photography, Writing, and Space in Shanghai, 1925–1937* (Durham, NC: Duke University Press, 2017), 257.

as Zhou Duo, incongruously displacing Surrealism's iconic fish amid an urban environment. Hence, these images will be analysed as part of Surrealism's artistic environment in Shanghai. Moreover Shi Zhecun, describes the work Pang Xunqin brought back from Paris as 'almost all Surrealist',[16] testifying to the range and reach of the movement in Shanghai. Yet, one of the most evident omissions relating to Surrealism's reception in the city are its three-dimensional forms.

Surrealism's theorisation of the object was only formalised in 1935, its sculptural oeuvre reaching its apogee in the 1930s. Consequently, the three-dimensional aspects of Surrealism most likely peaked too late for Shanghainese artists to digest before the outbreak of the Second Sino-Japanese War in 1937. Nevertheless, Surrealism in Shanghai became a multi-faceted movement that had a buoyancy and sphere of influence which has not been sufficiently explored.

The overarching historical context naturally shaped Surrealism's reception in the city. Undoubtedly, the May Fourth Movement of 1919, sparked off by a protest against China's response to the Treaty of Versailles was of primary significance. Here, in the wake of the First World War, imperial powers ruled that the former German Concession of Shandong be ceded to Japan by the Chinese government, a request that was complied with by the fledgling Beiyang government whose primary aim was to suppress internal strife amidst competing warlord factions.[17] As such, the May Fourth

16. Shi Zhecun, 'Milo de hua' [Miró's painting], in *Shi Zhecun qishinian wenxuan* (Shanghai: Shanghai wenyi chubanshe, 1996), 336.

17. The Beiyang government (1912–1928) was established after the fall of the Qing dynasty and its monarchy. It was initially run by military general Yuan Shikai until his death in 1916. Due to an ensuing power vacuum, the Beiyang

Movement responded to this national humiliation, catalysing the rejection of traditional Confucian values pertaining to obedience and a blossoming of individual rights enshrined in Western philosophy since the European Enlightenment. Whilst Surrealism itself did not conform to the values of the enlightenment, in the artistic domain, a small but significant number of Chinese artists began to study abroad, particularly in Paris and Japan where modernist currents including Surrealism were encountered directly.[18]

According to Huajing Xiu's PhD thesis, around 200 Chinese students studied abroad between 1912 and 1937, their primary destinations being Japan, France, the UK, the US, Belgium, Italy, and Switzerland.[19] This seems to be a primary route for Surrealism's emergence in Shanghai; students who had studied abroad founded avant-garde groups such as the aforementioned Storm Society and Chinese Independent Art Association upon their return to the city. Warlordism was largely eradicated in 1928 and China was ruled under Chiang Kai-shek's Nationalist Party, the *Guomindang*, in a decade of relative freedom which allowed for an expansion of culture despite the insipient threat of Japanese aggression.

Amid this historical backdrop, the idiosyncratic status of Shanghai was particularly conducive to artistic endeavour. As Zheng and Danzker, curators of the exhibition 'Shanghai Modern' in Munich (2004) put it:

government was beset by clashes between warlord factions before Chiang Kai-shek's Nationalist Party led the Northern Expedition between 1926 and 1928 ousting warlords and unifying China.

18. Most Japanese Surrealist artists had anti-establishment tendencies therefore it was not viewed as a contradiction to learn about Western avant-garde artistic movements from them.

19. Huajing Xiu, 'Shanghai–Paris: Chinese Painters in France and China, 1919–1937' (PhD thesis, University of Oxford, 2000), 74.

> One of the first global cities of the modern era: in the first decades of the 20th century a whirlpool of revolutionary ideas, conflicting nationalist aspirations, unrestrained commercial expansion and military occupation. A glittering *fata morgana*, by 1930 the fifth largest city in the world. Shanghai seduces and entices the imagination of the time.[20]

Shanghai became a breeding ground for cross-cultural influences primarily due to the enforced cosmopolitanism of two major trading ports leased to the imperial powers under duress, the Shanghai International Settlement and the French Concession, the latter becoming the cultural nexus of the city. Shanghai's French Concession (*La concession française de Shanghai*) was established as a treaty port in 1849 following China's defeat in the Opium Wars in 1842, in which the Qing dynasty tried and failed to ban the trading of this illicit and harmful substance that had cost many Chinese lives and livelihoods. During the 1920s and 1930s, the French Concession undoubtedly became the cultural epicentre of Shanghai, boasting the Shanghai Art College where nude drawing and Western painting were taught.

The founding of the Shanghai Art College (1913–1952) was strongly supported by the artist Liu Haisu whose pedagogical stance advocated that 'rejuvenating China's fine arts required engaging with and assimilating foreign trends of the time'.[21] As the detailed monograph by Shanghai studies scholar Jane Zheng reveals, the college was a private art

20. Jo-Anne Birnie Danzker, Ken Lum, and Shengtian Zheng, *Shanghai Modern: 1919–1945* (Ostfildern-Ruit: Hatje Cantz, 2004), 18.
21. Paul French, 'The Shanghai Academy of Art: The School that Gave the City Its Early 20th Century Aesthetic', *South China Morning Post*, 15 April 2021.

school with programs in both Western art and *guohua*.[22] Hence, hybrid interactions inevitably occurred between the two. Indeed, the Shanghai Art College hosted many teachers (Zhang Xian, Ni Yide, Pang Xunqin) and graduates (Zhou Duo, Duan Pingyou, Fu Lei) from the Storm Society who would utilise Surrealism in Shanghai.[23]

The college is perhaps best known for the fiasco surrounding the 'nude model incident'. The Shanghai Art College incorporated life drawing into the syllabus in 1920, which provoked moral controversy, the apotheosis of which was Liu Haisu's 'pen battle' with warlord Sun Chuanfang in 1926.[24] Conservative ideologies and those attributable to the relative social liberalism of a semi-colonial concession were pitted against each other. The nude features heavily among Shanghainese Surrealist -inspired artwork of the 1930s and would continue to incite debate. That said, the genre gradually became more accepted and regularly featured in the periodical press. It would seem that the gradual dissemination of the genre can be traced back to these debates of the 1920s held at the Shanghai Art College.

Shanghai's French Concession was also the home of numerous artists' studios and the French Jesuit L'Université de L'Aurore [Zhendan Daxue] where degree courses were taught in French alongside French language preparatory courses for study abroad. Moreover, burgeoning publishing houses and their pictorial magazines were abundant in this enclave due to relaxed rules surrounding censorship and the provision of a safe haven for political dissidents. Indeed, the French

22. See Jane Zheng, *The Modernization of Chinese Art: The Shanghai Art College, 1913–1937* (Leuven: Leuven University Press, 2016).
23. Zheng, *The Modernization of Chinese Art*, 134.
24. Zheng, *The Modernization of Chinese Art*, 106–7.

Concession was also home to the infamous gangster and leader of the 'Green Gang', Du Yuesheng, who ran illegal businesses such as prostitution and protection rackets in cahoots with the administrators of the French Concession while cooperating with them on the opium trade.[25] Furthermore, the first ever meeting of the Chinese Communist Party took place in Shanghai's French Concession in 1921. Among the delegates was a young Mao Zedong.

French historian Marie-Claire Bergère notes that in 1910 the population of the French Concession amounted to 116,000 inhabitants, 1,500 of these were foreign residents, the majority of whom were not French.[26] As such, the Concession formed a cosmopolitan convergence point of many cultures. Yet, in terms of architecture, the oft-cited nomenclature describing Shanghai as the 'Paris of the East', may well stem from what Bergère denotes as an 'exercise in urban planning and beautification, an exotic extension of the Haussmannian restructuring of Paris'.[27] Indeed, the Concession was renowned for its public parks, tree-lined streets, and wide avenues. In terms of governance, Bergère states that universal Jacobin values were promoted with Chinese citizens being granted access to most spaces which was more ahead of its time in comparison to the international concession.[28] The Concession was also synonymous with nightlife, parties, and leisure, home to the renowned

25. Zheng reveals Du was also on the school board of the Shanghai Art College! Zheng, *The Modernization of Chinese Art*, 125.
26. Marie-Claire Bergère, *Histoire de Shanghai* (Paris: Fayard, 2002).
27. Bergère, *Histoire de Shanghai.*
28. Bergère, *Histoire de Shanghai.*

Cercle Sportif Français, the French Club.[29] In short, the French Concession commingled the sordid with the sublime.

How then did Surrealism, an intrinsically anti-colonial movement, survive in an imperialist outpost? Firstly, it should be noted that with the threat of Japan's totalitarian form of imperialism on the horizon, the foreign concessions were generally looked upon as a lesser evil, though all forms of colonialism are, of course, inherently racist and exploitative. Secondly, the French Concession had the ability to subsume dissent much like mainland France itself. The original Parisian Surrealist grouping were notorious for their subversion of the French state. On 2 July 1925, the Surrealists infamously attended a banquet in honour of the Symbolist poet Saint-Pol-Roux. The gathering was largely comprised of the conservative literary elite. Here, the Surrealists distributed pamphlets against the French ambassador to Japan, Paul Claudel, who had attacked the movement.[30]

---

29. For more information on the Cercle Sportif Français, see my short article, L. Walden, 'Elite Cosmopolitanism in Shanghai's Former French Concession: The Cercle Sportif Français', *Visualising China*, University of Bristol, 2021, accessed 1 May 2024, https://visualisingchina.net/blog/2021/02/10/guest-blog-the-cercle-sportif-francais-elite-cosmopolitanism-in-shanghais-former-french-concession/.
30. Olivier Belin, 'Quand Le Banquet Tourne Mal: Les Surréalistes Contre Paul Claudel en 1925' [When the dinner didn't go down well: The Surrealists versus Paul Claudel in 1925], *Bulletin de La Société Paul Claudel* 225 (2018): 43–60. Claudel stated, 'In terms of recent movements, none will lead to any actual transformation or new creation, neither Dada nor Surrealism, which have only one meaning: pederasty', 45. Claudel held highly conservative religious and political beliefs. Moreover, in the tract the Surrealists distributed they state: 'We hope with all our being that the colonial revolutions, the wars and the insurrections will destroy Western civilization . . . We take this opportunity to publicly break with everything that is French, in words and deeds.' Irene Albers, 'The Surrealists' Anti-Colonialism', in Tom Holert, Franke Anselm, and Haus der Kulturen der Welt, *Neolithic Childhood: Art in a False Present c. 1930*, trans. Kevin Kennedy (Berlin: HKW Diaphanes, 2018), 244–47.

The Surrealists drew attention to the colonial enterprises Claudel was complicit in. Subsequently, a quarrel ensued between the guests and the Surrealist writer and ethnographer Michel Leiris shouted out of a window 'Long Live China' before affirming 'Down with France'.[31] This led to a street brawl with Leiris ironically only being saved from a lynching by the police.[32] Moreover, the expression of anti-colonial sentiment itself was not illegal in Shanghai's foreign concessions, both English- and French-language newspapers published such viewpoints as it was ultimately the official stance of the ruling Nationalist Party, despite their pragmatic alignments with the foreign concessions on numerous occasions.

Furthermore, it is possible that avant-garde art became an unintentional tool in reflecting the laissez-faire attitude of the French Concession towards prostitution, gambling, and opium smoking. While many artists intended to critique such an atmosphere, the visual reification of desire did little to attenuate the lure of a liberal enclave. These vices were tolerated in return for Du's Green Gang controlling Chinese citizens in the concession.[33] In short, the pluralism of the French Concession could countervail critique, including that of Surrealism. In fact, the *Journal de Shanghai* (1927–1945), the 'organ of French interests in the Far East' published the work of Storm Society painter Pang Xunqin in 1932 lauding

---

This adds weight to my argument that Surrealism should not necessarily be perceived as a Western movement, despite its Western origins.

31. Irene Albers, 'The Surrealists' Anti-Colonialism', 245.
32. Irene Albers, 'The Surrealists' Anti-Colonialism', 245.
33. Olivia Hunter, 'Crime and Security in Shanghai's French Concession 1919–1937', *Earlham Historical Journal* 9, no. 2 (2017): 114.

the fact that he had studied in Paris[34] in a fervent expression of 'Soft Power'.[35]

Despite the enforced nature of its establishment, Cinquini, a French art historian based in Shanghai, notes the cosmopolitan characteristics of the French Concession led to artistic experimentation during the Republican era (1911–1949),[36] stating: 'One should insist upon the particular features of the Shanghai French Concession as a space catalysing cultural relations between France and China as if Shanghai was playing the role of a melting pot, even a magic cauldron for Chinese artists searching for foreign influences to aid in national renewal.'[37] Indeed, following the impetus of the May Fourth Movement, the intention of certain Chinese artists was to pragmatically utilise Western iconography as a springboard to forge a new national identity at a time of political turbulence. Many artists who utilised Surrealism in China seem to align with the premise of 'grabbism' (*nalaizhuyi*) proposed by the modernist writer Lu Xun (1934).[38]

---

34. 'Quelques oeuvres du Peintre Chinois Hiunkin Pang' [Some works by the Chinese painter Pang Xunqin], *Le Journal de Shanghai*, 25 September 1932.
35. Political scientist Joseph Nye believed 'Soft Power' reflected the fact that 'proof of power lies not in resources but the ability to change the behaviour of states'. Joseph S. Nye, 'Soft Power', *Foreign Policy* 80 (1990): 153–71, 155.
36. The term 'Republican era' refers to the period between 1911 and 1949 after the overthrow of the last monarchical dynasty, the Qing, in 1911, until the Communist takeover of China in 1949.
37. Philippe Cinquini, 'Les artistes chinois en France et l'Ecole nationale supérieure des beaux-arts de Paris à l'époque de la Première République de Chine (1911–1949): pratiques et enjeux de la formation artistique académique' (Thesis, Université Charles-de-Gaulle – Lille 3, 2017), 33.
38. Lu Xun, 'Nalaizhuyi' [Grabbism], in *Zhongguo ribao* [China Daily], 7 June 1934. The phenomenon of 'grabbism' however, was clearly being practised by modern artists in Shanghai earlier than 1934 when Lu Xun first wrote about it. It should be stated that Lu Xun tended to favour left-wing socialist art rather than modernist works, but he wrote widely for magazines and newspapers

Lu Xun described China as isolated from other countries, espousing 'closed-ism' (*biguanzhuyi*). Instead, he demands a relationship of reciprocity between East and West, citing the fact that several Chinese antiquities have made their way to French museums,[39] therefore China should reciprocate by selectively extrapolating ideas from the West as opposed to passively receiving them. Lu Xun states that if ideas from the West are not 'grabbed', then Chinese culture will remain in a state of stagnation rather than becoming 'modern'. Several forms of cultural exchange in Republican China could be read as 'grabbism' due to their hybridity among which recourse to Surrealism seemed to be one of the most prominent choices amid several competing modernist currents.

Certainly, copious Shanghainese journals make mention of Surrealism as an aesthetic phenomenon and knowledge of the movement became widespread among well-informed artists. The earliest article dedicated to art-historical Surrealism, to my knowledge, appeared as a short column of the daily newspaper *Shenbao* [The Shun Pao] published on 4 June 1931.[40] In 1933, Ni Yide wrote a much more comprehensive article based on his understanding of Breton's

---

that most modernist artists would be acquainted with. Lu Xun actually criticised the modernist journal *Wenyi Huabao* [Literature and arts pictorial] which often featured Surrealist front covers. The journal editors stated they wanted to give the reader free rein rather than educate the masses. For more information on Lu Xun's critique of *Wenyi*, see Paul Bevan, *Intoxicating Shanghai: An Urban Montage: Art and Literature in Pictorial Magazines during Shanghai's Jazz Age* (Leiden: Brill, 2020), 143–57.

39. Some of course were illegally pillaged.

40. Xie Haiyan, 'Surrealist Painting', *Shenbao*, 6 April 1931. This assertion is predicated on a database search. References to numerous Shanghainese journals which acknowledged Surrealism (these are just examples) are woven throughout this text.

Le Surréalisme et la Peinture [Surrealism and painting].[41] Much later, as previously mentioned, a special edition of *Yifeng* magazine (1935) by the CIAA focused exclusively on Surrealism including the translation by Zhao Shou of the *Surrealist Manifesto*. It is clear therefore that artists who studied abroad and either read Japanese or French would have likely been acquainted with the manifesto much earlier. In the case of Zhao Shou, fellow CIAA member Liang Xihong reveals that he became interested in the *Surrealist Manifesto* around 1930,[42] when he was still a student in Guangzhou before studying abroad in Japan in 1933.[43] Indeed, the special edition talks about Surrealist concepts in significant depth.

The most lucid writing on Surrealism in China is ostensibly penned by CIAA member Li Dongping. For example, his article in *Yifeng* entitled 'Shenme Jiaozuo Chaoxianshizhuyi' [What is Surrealism?] discussed the movement in relation to

---

41. Ni Yide, 'Chaoxianshizhuyi de huihua' [Surrealist painting], *Yishu* [L'Art] 1 (1933). The text is referred to in more depth in the chapter 'Chinese Interpretations of European Surrealist Works'.
42. Liang Xihong, 'Chaoxianshizhuyi huajialun' [Theories of Surrealist painters], *Yifeng* [Art winds] 3, no. 10 (1935): 27–28.
43. Interestingly the fascinating article by Chen Qing, 'Yijie de lujing yu yiyi de zhuanhuan: lun Zhao Shou fanyi "Chaoxianshizhuyi xuanyan" Zhong de ji ge wenti' [Changing meanings through the process of translation: Discussing issues relating to Zhao Shou's translation of the Surrealist Manifesto], *Wenyi Yanjiu* 6 (2016): 122–31, argues that it is more likely Zhou Shou learnt some French while a student in Guangzhou and translated Breton's original manifesto rather than the Japanese version, particularly given none of the CIAA members complimented the Japanese school of Surrealism, a tendency attributed to fervent anti-Japanese sentiment at the time. While I do not believe enough concrete evidence is given to assert Zhao Shou definitely translated from the original French, what is certain is that Zhao Shou focused his translation on issues that resonated with Chinese traditional art. There is also the possibility that Zhao Shou translated the Surrealist Manifesto from a combination of the French and Japanese versions.

reality and dream. For Li Dongping, it is the porosity between these two phenomena which typifies the painterly expression of the movement. He comments that Surrealism 'freely distorts the object, eschewing the rules and constraints of the painting process, through the imagination, balancing consciousness with instinct, to take its current form'.[44]

Later, in 1936, an even more informed article is written by the same author for *Haibin Wenyi* [Seaside culture] entitled *Chaoxianshizhuyi qianqian houhou* [Surrealism before and after]. The article explores Surrealism in contradistinction to Dada which is criticised for its nihilistic, aloof approach to society. Freud is described as the 'scientific background' [*kexue beijing*] to Surrealism and an explanation of automatism [*zidongzhuyi*] is given.[45] However, no mention is made of Hegel, Marx, or the revolutionary, anti-nationalist aspects of the movement in any art journal to my knowledge. The only significant mention of the revolutionary aspects of Surrealism comes in 1932 through *Xiandai*, edited by Shi Zhecun. Here, in a piece entitled 'Faguo wenyi zazhi' [French literature and art periodicals], the author Gao Ming cites *La Révolution Surréaliste* (1924–1929) and *Le Surréalisme au Service de la Révolution* (1930–1933). He notes in relation to the latter that the group had turned towards Communism.[46] Chiang Kai-shek brutally purged communists from Shanghai

44. Li Dongping, 'Shenme Jiaozuo Chaoxianshizhuyi' [What is Surrealism?], *Yifeng* [Art winds] 3, no. 10 (1935): 27. Interestingly, the Chinese term for Surrealism literally means 'exceed reality-ism'.

45. Li Dongping, 'Chaoxianshizhuyi qianqian houhou' [Surrealism before and after], *Haibin Wenyi* [Seaside culture] Issue 2 (1936): 31–35.

46. In *Xiandai* [Les Contemporains] 4 (1932). For further detail, see Xu Jun and Song Xuezhi, 'Chaoxianshizhuyi zaizhongguo de yijie' [The translation and introduction of Surrealism in China], *Dangdai waiyuyanjiu* [Contemporary foreign language research] 2 (2010): 36–41.

in 1927 in cahoots with the authorities of the foreign concessions in an incident known as the Shanghai massacre.[47] As such, it was dangerous to show any form of sympathy with communist tendencies. For example, Shi Zhecun noted that during the two years he studied at L'Université de l'Aurore, his friend the author Dai Wangshu was arrested on suspicion of being a communist.[48] Therefore, many authors and artists may have chosen to self-censor the revolutionary aspects of Surrealism even if they were aware of them.

Despite this substantial evidence base, the negative views of certain scholars regarding Surrealism's influence in Shanghai such as art historian Ralph Crozier are difficult to overturn. He comments: 'It did not catch on in Shanghai, the centre of the Chinese art world.'[49] Crozier asserts that members of the Storm Society were 'experimenting in an effort to reach their own individual style, one could almost say ransacking the field of European Modernism'.[50] While there were several forms of modernism in the air in Shanghai at this juncture, many Chinese cultural and iconographic idiosyncrasies blended with Western techniques to catalyse a hybrid, cross-cultural form of artistic exchange. Moreover, in

47. Before the Shanghai Massacre of 1927, the Communist Party and Nationalist Party held a formal alliance, even receiving aid from the Soviet Union. Nationalist party leader, Chiang Kai-shek, concerned the Communist Party was gaining too much influence, having recently created a workers' commune in Shanghai, joined forces with the Foreign Concessions to stage a brutal massacre. This would lead to the ruralisation of the Chinese Communist Party.
48. See Shi Zhecun, 'Zhengdan liangnian' [Two years at Aurore University], in *Shi zhecun Qishinian wenxuan* (Shanghai: Shanghai wenyi chubanshe, 1996).
49. Ralph Crozier, 'Post-Impressionism in Pre-war Shanghai: The Juelanshe (Storm Society) and the Fate of Modernism in Republican China', in *Modernity in Asian Art*, ed. John Clark (Sydney: Wild Peony, 1993), 149.
50. Crozier, 'Post-Impressionism in Pre-war Shanghai', 146.

many cases, specifically Surrealist tendencies can be extrapolated from such artworks.

A more optimistic and nuanced author Paul Bevan counters 'the adoption of the visual world of Surrealism by so many artists in the art world in China has not been widely recognised by art historians and consequently has not found a place in the standard art history books'.[51] Bevan has assiduously interrogated the presence of Surrealism vis-à-vis Shanghai cartoonists, identifying an expanded locus of Surrealist activity in Shanghai including the widespread use of Surrealist cartoons as marginalia to modernist short stories.[52] In Bevan's *Intoxicating Shanghai* (2020), he advocates for the unacknowledged importance of pictorial magazines *Wenyi* and *Wanxiang* in the propagation of Surrealism in China.[53] Yet, Bevan does caveat his work on this phenomenon, noting 'In China it is not possible to identify a Surrealist movement as such.'[54] Indeed, there was no single Surrealist movement in Republican China, but this volume asserts the presence of a culturally specific Chinese Surrealism as a widely disseminated force that reacted to both the sociopolitical context of Republican China and the artistic impetus for hybridity in Shanghai's French Concession.

Regrettably, the vast majority of avant-garde activity in Shanghai ceased at the outbreak of the Sino-Japanese War in 1937. As such, Surrealism in Shanghai succumbed to external circumstances, its ephemeral lifespan explaining the reluctance of many academics to accept it as an important

51. Paul Bevan, *A Modern Miscellany: Shanghai Cartoon Artists, Shao Xunmei's Circle and the Travels of Jack Chen 1926–1938* (Leiden: Brill, 2016), 237.
52. Bevan, *A Modern Miscellany*, 237.
53. Bevan, *Intoxicating Shanghai*, 66–69.
54. Bevan, *Intoxicating Shanghai*, 356.

movement in modern China. Therefore, in this multi-layered context of a Republican Shanghai and the cosmopolitan, yet semi-colonial enclave of the French Concession, I explore the Surrealist -leaning avant-garde groupings of the Storm Society and Chinese Independent Art Association, while also considering how these entities conceived of European Surrealist painting. A case study of Pang Xunqin, co-founder of the Storm Society, who encountered Surrealism first-hand in Paris, is equally elaborated. Exploring both the Freudian and latent Marxist aspects of Surrealism in Shanghai, we turn to *Xiandai* magazine (1932–1935). In relation to Surrealist photography in China, satirical photomontages in the prominent periodical *Modern Sketch* are analysed and a case study of photographer Lang Jingshan, who garnered his inspiration from the Surrealist photographer Man Ray, is made.

On a conceptual level, I hope to demonstrate that Surrealism in Shanghai assumed a dialectical form similar to the Parisian movement, something also intrinsic to China's indigenous religion of Daoism although the latter espoused harmony as opposed to conflictual resolution. Daoism's relationship with Surrealism reached its apotheosis during the 1950s after the devastation of Second World War (1939–1945). At this juncture, non-Western thought was instrumentalised by the Surrealists as a form of spiritual rejuvenation, while the Daoist notion of *wuwei* (non-action) aligned with Surrealist automatism or the idea of creating without forethought. Nevertheless, evidence shows that many Surrealists were cognisant of Daoism at a formative stage of their careers.

French Surrealist painter André Masson's knowledge of Daoism preceded his knowledge of Surrealism itself, first encountering Laozi's *Dao de jing* [Book of Changes] in

1913.[55] As early as 1936, his paintings, along with those of Joan Miró, were featured in Georges Duthuit's 1936 book *Chinese Mysticism and Modern Painting*. As opposed to their controversial reception in Europe, Duthuit comments of the Surrealists that 'there can be no doubt that they would in no way have baffled a cultured Chinese, that is to say a man whose forefathers were the first to track down and explore the fugitive lands of the imagination'.[56] The journal *La Révolution Surréaliste* [The Surrealist revolution] published an article by the German philosopher Theodor Lessing entitled 'L'Europe et L'Asie' [Europe and Asia] (1925), which also references the Daoist idea of *wuwei*, contrasted with the opposite impetus common to European philosophy. During the 1920s and 1930s the French Surrealist playwright and poet Antonin Artaud also acknowledged the Daoist doctrine of *wuwei* as well as the notion of the void. He imagined himself reincarnated as Lao Zi (Lao Tzu) while interned at a psychiatric hospital believing he had lived 5,000 years ago in a conflation of temporality.[57]

Surrealist ethnographer Michel Leiris states: 'It was at the time of the beginnings of Surrealism that I read the *Tao Te Ching* when, like my companions, I was looking towards Asia as a symbol of knowledge plunging into the night of time, just as Black Africa and Oceania would soon seem to me symbols of a primitiveness also calculated to ruin Western logic, a logic that had succeeded in engendering

---

55. Marguerite Hui Müller-Yao, *The Influence of Chinese Calligraphy on Western Informal Painting* (Hamburg: Dietger Müller, 2015), 192.
56. Georges Duthuit, *Chinese Mysticism and Modern Painting* (Paris: Chroniques du jour; London: A. Zwemmer 1936), 24.
57. Florence de Mèredieu, *La Chine d'Antonin Artaud* [The China of Antonin Artaud] (Paris: Blusson, 2006), 60.

only coercion and machines.'[58] This statement is of course couched in an Orientalist frame of reference, but demonstrates from the very beginnings of Surrealism, Daoism was seen to overturn Western rationality. Both the *Daodejing* and Surrealism assert the primacy of dialectic thought. The *Daodejing* (c. 400 BC) foundational text of Daoism, professes: 'difficulty and ease produce the one (the idea of) the other; that length and shortness fashion out the one the figure of the other; that (the ideas of) height and lowness arise from the contrast of the one with the other'.[59] This very much resembles the statement in Surrealism's second manifesto (1929) that 'Everything tends to make us believe that there exists a certain point of the mind at which life and death, the real and the imagined, past and future, the communicable and the incommunicable, high and low, cease to be perceived as contradictions,'[60] which became known in Surrealism as the 'supreme point'. As such, Daoism's symbiosis with Surrealism from its inception catalyses my questioning of Surrealism's art historiography as an intrinsically Western movement. These views are echoed by Chinese artists themselves apropos the purported originality of Surrealism. Indeed, the British-based Chinese poet, painter, and traveller Chiang Yee (aka 'The Silent Traveller') stated in 1938:

> there is essentially nothing new in Surrealism to the Chinese mind, accustomed through many centuries to an attitude of receptivity towards purely linear beauty, its principles cause no shock. A piece of our most ancient script composed perhaps 5000 years ago, and a Surrealist

58. Michel Leiris and Lydia Davis, *Fibrils* (New Haven: Yale University Press, 2017), 6.
59. Lao Zi, *Tao te Ching*, trans. James Legge (n.p.: Standard Ebooks, 2021), 52.
60. Breton, *Manifestoes of Surrealism*, 123.

drawing of the twentieth century produce very similar aesthetic emotions.[61]

Indeed, the blurring of dream and reality has always been a fundamental notion of traditional Chinese art, realism largely assuming the form of a Western import in the early twentieth century, to counter the subjectivity of Chinese literati painting which 'monopolised the discourse on art in imperial China'.[62]

I theorise that through the dialectic and its resonances with Chinese traditional thought, Surrealism was able to subsume Shanghai's multifarious contradictions of East/West, colonial/cosmopolitan, ancient/modern. This was achieved through eschewing the boundaries of reality and dream, the individual psyche of the artist processed these contradictions and reified them in a visual form. This is not to say that Chinese Surrealists rigidly followed their Parisian counterparts. Rather than viewing Surrealism through a universalist lens, I hope to posit for the cultural specificity of the movement in Shanghai which, from an aesthetic standpoint often commingled Surrealist techniques and elements of traditional Chinese iconography. From a structural angle, this study emphasises that rather than revolving around one core group with a leader where a quasi-formal membership was required à la Breton, Surrealism in Shanghai was much more diffuse, traversing different periodicals, avant-garde groupings, and even political ideologies ranging from Nationalist to Communist.

61. Chiang Yee, *Chinese Calligraphy: An Introduction to Its Aesthetic and Technique*, third revised and enlarged edition (Cambridge, MA: Harvard University Press, 1973), 108.

62. Cheng-Hua Wang, 'Rediscovering Song Painting for the Nation: Artistic Discursive Practices in Early Twentieth-Century China', *Artibus Asiae* 71, no. 2 (2011): 225.

PANG XUNQIN AND THE STORM SOCIETY

Pang Xunqin was an artist whose work began firmly situated in the Freudian basis of Surrealism but as tensions with Japan rose, his work would culminate in a more revolutionary engagement with the movement. Pang belonged to a highly select coterie of Chinese artists who imbibed Surrealist artworks first-hand through an extensive period of study abroad in Paris between 1925 and 1929. This is significant as his stay coincides with the first stage of Surrealism's artistic flourishing in Paris. He then returned to Shanghai, founding the 'Storm Society' in 1932, which formally acknowledged the 'desires of Surrealism[1] in their manifesto. During the short lifespan of the Storm Society between 1932 and 1935, I argue that Surrealism became the primary source of influence upon Pang Xunqin's works.

Pang's experiences amid the cosmopolitan metropoles of Paris and Shanghai are recounted in his 1988 autobiography *Jiushi zheyang zouguolaide* [Such was the path I travelled].[2] His artistic yearnings began at the Université de

1. *Yishu Xunkan* [Art trimonthly] 1, no. 5 (1932): 8.
2. Pang Xunqin, *Jiushi zheyang zouguolaide* [Such was the path I travelled] (Beijing: Shenghuo, dushu, xinzhi sanlian shudian, 2005).

l'Aurore in Shanghai's French Concession, a francophone Catholic establishment led by a group of Jesuit priests where his desire to travel to France had undoubtedly been cultivated. Pang's mother encouraged him to apply to the university in 1921 with the rationale: 'Many people speak English, but few can speak French,'[3] hoping her son could distinguish himself in what was, at the time, the fifth largest city in the world with roughly three million inhabitants.

Despite the somewhat austere nature of L'Aurore, a priest spotted Pang's artistic talent and gave him American photography magazines including nude models to peruse, somewhat uncharacteristic of a religious establishment.[4] Chinese society had (and still has) a very conservative attitude towards nudity, the painting of nude models (*luoti*) at the Shanghai Art College famously being banned in 1926 by the conservative warlord Sun Chuanfang, de facto warlord ruler over Shanghai at the time before the Nationalist Party took over.[5] In spite of the colonial imposition of French culture in Shanghai via the Concession, it is clear that Pang equated Western art with notions of freedom in contradistinction to what was perceived by many Chinese avant-garde artists as the unyielding, millennia-old tradition of *guohua* or national painting, the mainstream Chinese form of expression at the time, broadly limited in scope to landscapes and the natural world.[6] Indeed, Pang had spoken out

3. Pang, *Jiushi zheyang zouguolaide*, 25.
4. Pang, *Jiushi zheyang zouguolaide*, 34.
5. See Jane Zheng, *The Modernization of Chinese Art: The Shanghai Art College, 1913–1937* (Leuven: Leuven University Press, 2016), 106–14.
6. It should, however, be noted that certain artists intuited Surrealist elements in Chinese *guohua* which were by no means an elegy to imported Western realist ideals, some of which are explored in this volume. According to Zheng's, *The Modernisation of Chinese Art*, there is an article by Bao Xiling

against 'literati' culture.[7] Conversely, Pang became enthralled by various strands of modernism that were slowly infiltrating Shanghai's colonial cityscape during the late 1920s.

Here, I hope to illuminate Pang's artistic trajectory from a student in Paris to a practitioner in Shanghai. Pang undertook a journey from assimilation to hybridity, from a reliance on Western norms and the self-effacement of his Chinese identity in Paris, to his unique use of Surrealist techniques commingled with Chinese iconography upon his return to Shanghai, embodying Cinquini's notion of the French Concession as a 'magic cauldron' of creation. Indeed, as Sullivan notes of Chinese artists in Paris in 1959, 'Nearly all artists became western painters . . . but in a few individual cases individual talent enabled the artist to escape an abject capitulation to the *beaux arts* tradition.'[8] Ultimately, Pang's unique Chinese Surrealist style would only fully blossom upon his return to Shanghai where he embodied postcolonial theorist Homi K. Bhabha's notion of 'Vernacular Cosmopolitanism'. For Bhabha, Cosmopolitanism is an empirical facet of everyday life defined as 'moving in-between

---

entitled 'Zhongguohua de chaoxianshixing' [The Surrealistic properties of Chinese national paintings], in *Shanghai meishuzhuan xinzhi di sishi biye jiniankan* [The fourteenth yearbook of the Shanghai Art College] (publication details not cited in Zheng's book, 1932), 155–57, on this theme. See Zheng, 377. The commingling of Surrealism with traditional Chinese painting is explored further in the work of Zeng Ming, Zhao Shou, and the chapter 'Chinese Interpretations of European Surrealist Works'.

7. Pang Xunqin, 'Tan hua' [On painting], *Liuyi* [The six arts] vol. 1, no. 1 (15 February 1936): 35–36. For more on this subject, consult the forthcoming article by Paul Bevan entitled 'Surrealism and the Manhua Artists of Liuyi', in the *Journal of Contemporary Chinese Art*, Issue 11.23 (2024).

8. Michael Sullivan, *Chinese Art in the Twentieth Century* (Berkeley: University of California Press, 1959), 58. Sullivan is a renowned scholar and major collector of Chinese art. His collection is now housed in the Ashmolean Museum, University of Oxford.

cultural traditions and revealing hybrid forms of life and art that do not have a prior existence within the discrete world of any single culture or language'.[9] This is enacted by Pang's distinctly Surrealist *and* Shanghainese repertoire of distorted nudes, phantasmal cityscapes, and political dystopia. Pang also manifested a Surrealist sense of 'Le merveilleux quotidien' [The everyday marvellous],[10] where he transformed daily ephemera such as streetlamps, playing cards, and coffee shops into art, in keeping with his Parisian peers.

His first year of preparatory university education at L'Aurore was broad and included pencil drawing classes, however, in his autobiography, Pang draws attention to the somewhat pragmatic nature of this endeavour, commenting: 'These pencil drawing classes were intended to relate to our future majors. Medics would draw bones, muscles, internal organs etc. Engineers would draw works of civil engineering, machinery and electrical appliances. It was aimed at helping our future study rather than becoming a painter.'[11] After his preparatory year, Pang entered the medical school of the university but quickly became disillusioned with his career choice and decided to become a painter instead. In the winter of 1924, he encountered another priest to whom

9. Sullivan, *Chinese Art in the Twentieth Century*, xviii.
10. In *Le Paysan de Paris* (1926), Louis Aragon attempts to grasp a sense of the 'marvellous everyday' by wandering through the streets of Paris, particularly the Passage de L'Opéra. His phrase the 'marvellous everyday' is coined in the first section of the novel, a 'Preface to a Modern Mythology'. As such the 'marvellous everyday' is viewed as an integral part of what it means to be modern, with street signs and café price lists strewn throughout the narrative, daily ephemera hence transformed into art. Aragon defines the marvellous as 'La contradiction qui apparaît dans le reel' [The contradiction that appears within reality]. As such, the 'marvellous everyday' refers to phenomena which distort reality while remaining an integral part of daily life.
11. Pang, *Jiushi zheyang zouguolaide*, 30.

he admitted this desire. He was met with the response: 'To be honest, you Chinese, you won't be able to become great painters.'[12] Confronted with such ingrained prejudice, rather than becoming dispirited, Pang decided to leave the university to study painting under a Russian artist before purchasing a third-class ticket for a mail boat headed for Paris in August 1925. André Breton's Surrealist movement had formally emerged in the city only a year beforehand. Breton's manifesto of 1924 exalted the notion of psychic freedom[13] that Pang had yearned for, noting in his biography that China was not predisposed to such a notion as freedom [*ziyou*],[14] due to its feudal past and colonial present. This observation was provoked after Pang was arbitrarily beaten up by an evidently racist British solider in the international settlement of the colonial metropolis. As such, Pang wanted to explore whether the notion of freedom existed in any country.

Arriving in Paris, Pang decided to enter the Académie Julian, which boasted notable Surrealist luminaries such as Jean Arp and Marcel Duchamp. Pang bestowed both praise and criticism on the institution in equal proportion, stating that: 'Teachers only come in once a week and will only critique oil paintings,' however he also 'received many people's help and progressed quickly.' All in all, Pang believed that it was through the help of his peers, rather

12. Pang, *Jiushi zheyang zouguolaide*, 36.
13. André Breton, *Manifestoes of Surrealism*, trans. Richard Seaver and Helen R. Lane (Ann Arbor: University of Michigan Press, 1969), 4. 'The mere word "freedom" is the only one that still excites me. I deem it capable of indefinitely sustaining the old human fanaticism. It doubtless satisfies my only legitimate aspiration. Amongst the many misfortunes to which we are heir, it is only fair to admit that we are allowed the greatest degree of freedom of thought.'
14. Pang, *Jiushi zheyang zouguolaide*, 38.

than teachers, that his painting improved, commenting 'large-group teaching should be implemented in order to let students mutually help each other'.[15] One of the other principal benefits of studying at Julian was that Pang rapidly expanded his social network, and in light of his doubts surrounding the pedagogy of the academy, was persuaded by a fellow Chinese artist, Chang Yu, to switch to the Académie de la Grande Chaumière in Montparnasse.

Chang Yu (professionally known as Sanyu) came to Paris in 1921 following a wave of Chinese migrating to the city through work-study programmes sponsored by the Chinese government. Sanyu, however, was not bound by such restrictions, financially supported by his wealthy brother Chang Jumin who owned a silk factory. After Jumin passed away in 1931, Sanyu's stipend abruptly stopped, and he eked out a bohemian existence in Paris. In a common cliché, he only garnered significant attention posthumously after his untimely passing in 1966. Rather than return to China where he could have found a prestigious position in an art academy like many of his peers, Sanyu chose to remain in his adopted city.[16] Pang had great admiration for Sanyu, who most likely drew the Surrealist muse Kiki of Montparnasse. Indeed, in Kiki's autobiography she commented that she would soon have to learn Chinese.[17] Moreover, Sanyu had himself been drawn by Picasso. Ruminating on Sanyu's nudes, Wang notes

15. Pang, *Jiushi zheyang zouguolaide*, 47.
16. For a more in-depth biography of Sanyu, consult Rita Wong, 'Sanyu Biography', Li Ching Cultural and Educational Foundation, accessed 1 May 2024, https://www.sanyu.org/biography.php?lang=en. Wong also details the reason Chang Yu was known as Sanyu, related to the Sichuan dialect pronunciation of his name.
17. Rita Wong, *Sanyu Catalogue Raisonnée: Drawings and Watercolours* (Taipei: Li Ching Cultural and Educational Foundation, 2014), 27.

'cursive drawing enacts the Surrealist aspiration toward automatism as a way of articulating the inner urges'.[18,19] Indeed, Chang Yu's hallmark comprised line drawings of the female form, conjoining an ancient Chinese artistic technique with Surrealist automatism, a practice he imparted to Pang, encouraging him to draw nude models at Chaumière. In a work Pang produced between 1930 and 1934 upon his return to Shanghai, Sanyu's inspiration is evident, the cursive line dominating the canvas. Both artworks cannot be ascribed any sense of cultural specificity, instead they firmly reside in the realm of the hybrid whereby 'Hybridity refers to the character of particular expressive forms that emerge from cultural synthesis.'[20] In other words, these works are idiosyncratic to Chinese painters who were also au fait with Surrealism.

Regularly attending La Grande Chaumière, Pang writes at length about the atmosphere of Montparnasse in his autobiography, in particular the café culture prevalent at the time:

> Coffee shops were not simply a place to drink coffee, they were a site of cultural activities, not only painters and sculptors, but also authors, poets, critics and socialites such as Kiki frequented them. The past few years have centred on Le Dôme. Now, the centre of activity has moved to La Coupole.[21]

---

18. Co-founder of the Storm Society Ni Yide described Chinese line drawing as 'Surrealistic' since it was 'weak at artistic representation'; see Zheng, *The Modernization of Chinese Art*, 233.
19. Eugene Wang, 'Sanyu ou un surréaliste chinois à Paris: Sanyu: A Chinese Surrealist in Paris', *Sanyu: l'écriture du corps: Language of the Body* (Paris: ARAA/Skira, 2004), 61–65.
20. Steven Leuthold, *Cross-Cultural Issues in Art: Frames for Understanding* (New York: Routledge, 2011), 26.
21. Pang, *Jiushi zheyang zouguolaide*, 72.

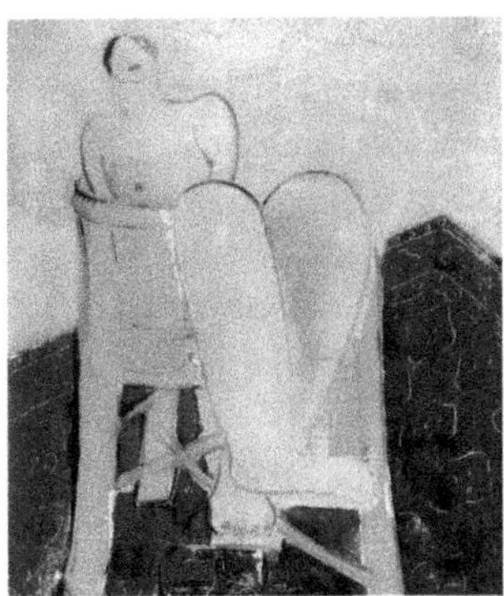

Figure 2. Pang Xunqin (1930–1934), *Body on Wicker Chair* (oil on canvas), 100 × 81 cm. Courtesy of Pang Hiunkin (Pang Xunqin) Archives at the Li Ching Cultural and Educational Foundation.

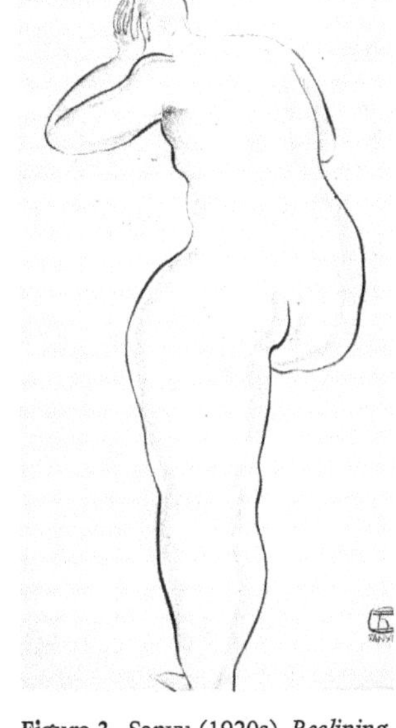

Figure 3. Sanyu (1920s), *Reclining Beauty Kiki of Montparnasse* (ink on paper), 44.5 × 27 cm. Courtesy of the Li Ching Cultural and Educational Foundation.

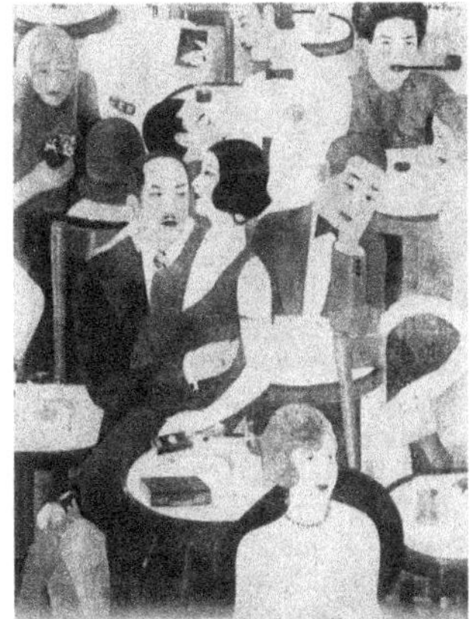

Figure 4. Pang Xunqin (1930), *The Café* (reproduction of oil painting, work lost), in *Nanhua Wenyi* 1, no. 15 (1932) (front cover). Courtesy of Pang Hiunkin (Pang Xunqin) Archives at the Li Ching Cultural and Educational Foundation.

This is a viewpoint mirrored by art historian Sue Roe who notes: 'The opening of La Coupole on 20 December 1927 identified Montparnasse not only as the hub of daytime café life but also as the fashionably arty locus of Parisian actresses, journalists, writers and artists including Cocteau, Man Ray (with Kiki de Montparnasse, and other adoring women).' Pang created copious vistas of Parisian café culture including a work called *Kafeidian* (The Café) (Fig. 4). Unfortunately, Pang destroyed many of his works made in Paris,[22] however a black and white reproduction can be found in the periodical *Nanhua Wenyi* [Culture and art of southern China]. In their PhD thesis, Zhu Xiaoqing interviewed Pang Xunqin's daughter Pang Tao about the work who recalled: 'quite a few figures were depicted in the work. Kiki, the famed muse for the artists of Montparnasse, was in the middle, sitting on the lap of a male artist, and Pang Xunqin put himself at the back of the crowds'.[23] While it is difficult to extrapolate idiosyncratic Surrealist traits from this painting, it nevertheless testifies to the social circles Pang gained access to alongside his assimilation of the Surrealist and modernist trope of the muse embodied by Kiki. Kiki de Montparnasse, the moniker of Alice Prin, was raised in poverty began work life-modelling

22. During the Cultural Revolution (1966–1976), paintings situated outside the prescribed style of Socialist Realism were generally banned and evidence of owning such paintings could provide evidence of counter-revolutionary activity. As such, for his own self-protection, Pang Xunqin destroyed many of his Surrealist works both made in Paris and China during the Cultural Revolution while many others were lost in the chaos of the Sino-Japanese War or simply given to his friends before he left Paris.
23. Xiaoqing Zhu, 'Pang Xunqin (1906–1985): A Chinese Avant-Garde's Metamorphosis, 1925–1946, and Questions of "Authenticity"' (PhD diss., University of Maryland, 2009), 46, accessed on 1 May 2024, http://hdl.handle.net/1903/9904.

for sculptors, which led to her mother disowning her. She soon gained renown and posed for many avant-garde artists in Paris. She was in a fiery relationship with Surrealist photographer Man Ray between 1921 and 1929. Besides being an artists' muse, Kiki was a painter in her own right, although her works have yet to receive the attention of those by the male painters who depicted her. Pang's self-positioning at the background of the canvas perhaps serves as a metaphor for his attitude towards the Parisian Surrealists at this juncture, languishing somewhere on the fringes of their activity and never formally being accepted into or acknowledged by their grouping. While the black and white reproduction impedes a detailed formal analysis, it is clear here that Pang is operating in an assimilationist modality, fully ensconced in the Parisian school of painting. In fact, the work manifests a quasi-commercial quality, reminiscent of Toulouse Lautrec's Post-Impressionist style. Indeed, at this stage Pang had yet to develop specifically Surrealist tendencies and was still experimenting with multiple currents of Western modernism.

Notwithstanding, while at Chaumière, Pang created a work called *Death* [*Si*] (1928). His peers immediately noted its Surrealist qualities: 'Some people thought this was the flourishing of Surrealist philosophy. Whilst I affirm that my painting did go down that route, I didn't feel that the work should belong to a particular art movement.'[24] Indeed, we must readily admit that Pang Xunqin also had a fondness for Cubism while in Paris, mainly due to his admiration for Picasso, who both the Cubists and Surrealists simultaneously claimed as one of their own. In the Shanghai magazine *Yishu Xunkan* [L'Art], where Pang regularly published writings

24. Pang, *Jiushi zheyang zouguolaide*, 81.

about modern art, he waxes lyrical on the morality of imitation and the genius of Picasso, someone he clearly emulated in his work *Mother and Son* (Fig. 5) which incorporates the geometric reductivity and anatomical distortions symptomatic of this artist's oeuvre. Pang states: 'Sometimes a painting can clearly manifest one's own artistic style and concept, however, imitating x and y has always been necessary, in this way, a painting becomes a new genre. Oil painters imitated Cezanne, Renoir, and Picasso to death.'[25]

On a theoretical level, Pang is couching his complete assimilation into French schools of painting as a gateway to hybridity, advocating for the palimpsest-like qualities of artistic style, originality being a chimerical notion at best. This is a principle supported by art historian John Clark who theoretically sketches the sequelae of assimilation in his book *Modern Asian Art*: 'When assimilation is complete there are often radical attempts to transform a transferred technique by its deployment of subject matter or technical developments unknown or barely given prominence in the discourse from which the transfer came.'[26] In other words, Pang believed it was first necessary to completely immerse himself in French modernist painting, both in terms of style and subject matter, before innovating these borrowings into his own individual voice.

The aforementioned Surrealist work *Death* only exists as a very poor black and white reproduction to accompany an article in *Zhonghua ribao* [Central China Daily News]

25. 'Yishu Xunkan' [L'Art], *Xunqin suibi di si qi* [Pang Xunqin's writings number 4], 2 (1932): 10.
26. John Clark, *Modern Asian Art* (Honolulu: University of Hawaii Press, 1998), 24.

by art critic Sun Fuxi,[27] who reviewed Pang Xunqin's solo exhibition in 1932. Notwithstanding, in his autobiography Pang provides us with a description that nevertheless affirms the Surrealist qualities of *Death*: 'The subtitle of the painting was: only in death can all suffering be eliminated . . . there is no specific image in this painting, only a triangle positioned at a 45-degree angle, a mountain range pattern shaped like a dog's tooth, undulating ripples, and a vortex emanating out of a black dot.'[28] Here, it is clear that Pang drew from the Surrealist penchant for incongruous juxtaposition which reified the premise of reconciling opposing forces. *Death* also appears to draw from the dreamscape in order to depict the 'setbacks we all face in life',[29] arguing death is the only release from such a tumultuous agglomeration of shapes and motifs that resemble a highly fraught microcosm of lived experience. Moreover, Sun Fuxi provides us with further details on this particular artwork, noting that Pang told him that his intention was to deform and reform natural shapes, very much correlating with Surrealist processes of distorting reality.[30]

Linkages between Surrealism and death are copious, given many of its protagonists fought in the First World War. Similarly, Pang had lived through many cataclysmic events in Chinese history such as the Xinhai revolution, in

---

27. Sun Fuxi was an important cultural figure in both artistic and literary fields during the Republican era. He studied abroad in Lyon, France, between 1921 and 1925, before returning to China. He would go on to found the influential *Yifeng* [Art winds] periodical which published a special issue on Surrealism in 1935.
28. Pang, *Jiushi zheyang zouguolaide*, 81.
29. Pang, *Jiushi zheyang zouguolaide*, 81.
30. Sun Fuxi, 'Jieshao Pang Xunqin de huazhan' [Introducing Pang Xunqin's exhibition], *Zhonghua ribao* [Central China Daily News], 15 September 1932, 7.

which the last monarchical dynasty of the Qing was overthrown (1911), warlordism (1916–1928), and the Shanghai Massacre (1927) where communists were killed in foreign concessions by nationalist forces. In particular, Hal Foster, whose work focuses on linkages between the avant-garde and the postmodern, notes of Surrealism's reification of Freud's death-drive: 'Breton first intuited the existence of a psychic surreality on the basis of soldiers *délires aigus*, i.e., symptoms of shock, of traumatic neurosis, of scenes of death compulsively restaged.'[31] The motivations behind Pang's first Surrealist work certainly seem to reside in this same means to catharsis.

Despite demonstrating affinities with Surrealism during his Parisian years, Pang wished to attenuate his inevitable propensity towards the aesthetic assimilation of Western modernist norms and regain his artistic autonomy. As Zhu Xiaoqing notes: Pang 'was increasingly overwhelmed by a flood of avant-garde currents connected with L'École de Paris and simultaneously struggling in search of his own voice. He was torn between staying in Paris or returning to China'.[32] After four years in Paris, Pang decided to return home in 1929. Indeed, it is ostensibly when Pang develops his own hybrid style of Chinese Surrealism back in Shanghai that his own artistic vision was finally found.

In 1932, Pang Xunqin founded the Storm Society with Ni Yide, a strong advocate of Surrealism who had encountered the movement in Japan, writing several essays on the subject. The pair had met while teaching at the Shanghai Art College. The manifesto of the Storm Society directly

31. Hal Foster, *Compulsive Beauty* (Cambridge, MA: MIT Press, 1993), 1.
32. Zhu, 'Pang Xunqin (1906–1985)', 50.

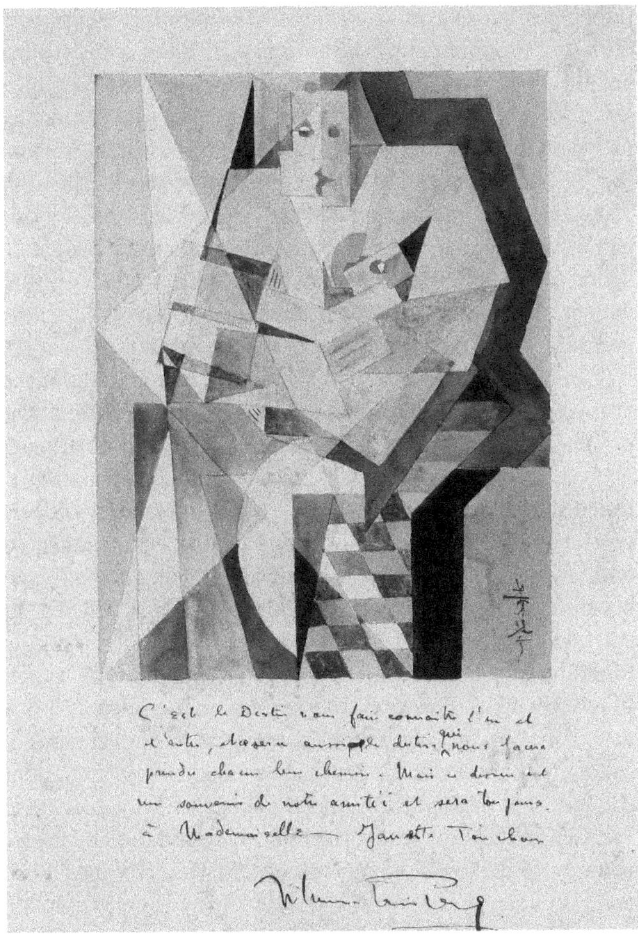

Figure 5. Pang Xunqin (1927), *Mother and Son* (watercolour on paper). Private collection. Courtesy of Pang Hiunkin (Pang Xunqin) Archives at the Li Ching Cultural and Educational Foundation.

references Surrealism as a source of inspiration whilst concurrently propounding: 'The art world in 20th century China should also foster this new atmosphere. Let's us rise up'.[33] By 1932, China had already transitioned from a monarchy to a fledgling republic that dissolved into a warlord era, and finally to a unified nationalist regime and was under threat of Japanese invasion due to the Manchurian Crisis.[34] It is in this turbulent social context that the Storm Society was established. While explicitly referring to the desires of Surrealism, it is probable that the Storm Society also drew from the political, revolutionary aspects of the movement.

In his autobiography, Pang couches the founding of the Storm Society in the aftermath of the 'January 28th' incident of 1932 where a crowd of Chinese had attacked a nationalist sect of Japanese Buddhist priests in Shanghai's international settlement due to high-ranking Japanese army officers disobeying orders, resulting in one death. Japan retaliated with an aerial bombardment of Shanghai. Pang had suffered because of the incident, his friend, a pilot, was killed.[35] As such, political turmoil was undoubtedly a catalyst for the founding of the Storm Society, which, I would argue, aimed to relate a revolution in art to a revolution in society.

Therefore, it is important to emphasise both the political context and aesthetic resonances enacted by Pang under the auspices of the Storm Society. First, we turn to two of Pang's Surrealist art works that have received the most commentary: a deliberate juxtaposition of two cityscapes: *Such*

33. *Yishu Xunkan* [Art trimonthly] 1, no. 5 (1932). 8.
34. The Manchurian Crisis refers to an event in which the Japanese deliberately bombed their own railway line and subsequently blamed the Chinese as a pretext to invade and colonise this northern province of China.
35. Pang, *Jiushi zheyang zouguolaide*, 129.

Is Paris and *Such Is Shanghai* (Figs 6 and 7), both of which embody Louis Aragon's notion of the everyday marvellous, situated in the reality of the cityscape while actively distorting it at the same time. *Such Is Paris* (1931) creates a Surrealist pastiche of the city, which superimposes socialites smoking, gambling, drinking, and dancing. A homage to Marcel Duchamp's *Fountain* (1917)[36] can be found in the bottom right-hand corner. Moreover, this is also a painting that depicts the cosmopolitanism of Paris during the 1920s with multiple ethnicities included in the composition. Conversely, *Such Is Shanghai* [Original title: *The Riddle of Life*] is a much more sombre work, ensconced in the underbelly of Shanghai nightlife, indeed, gestures towards prostitution abound due to the connotations of flowers signifying availability in Chinese culture.[37] The work is riddled with hedonism, materialism, vice, and gambling, all of which could be couched as colonial impositions. The Surrealist attributes of this painting are well summarised by art historian Jenny Lin: 'The watercolour also integrates artistic tactics aligned with the French Surrealist artworks and writings Pang Xunqin had studied, such as the transformation of everyday objects into occult symbols, the creation of a diaphanous, oneiric tableau, and the picturing of chances lost in the modern city through the figure of the enigmatic woman.'[38] *Such Is Shanghai* was

36. Zhu, 'Pang Xunqin (1906–1985)'. Duchamp's *Fountain* is too early to be classed as Surrealist although it does have Surrealist qualities in the sense of the objet trouvé (found object). Throughout his career that defied classification, Duchamp's oeuvre transcended the confines of avant-garde groupings. However, he would collaborate with the Surrealists on many occasions, in particular for their International Surrealist Exhibitions.

37. Jenny Lin, *Above Sea: Contemporary Art, Urban Culture, and the Fashioning of Global Shanghai* (Manchester: Manchester University Press, 2018).

38. Lin, *Above Sea.*

exhibited at Pang Xunqin's solo exhibition held in Shanghai at L'Aurore in 1932 where he had previously studied to be a medic. Commenting on this exhibition in *Yishu Xunkan,* Fu Lei, Francophile author and translator, anchored this work within the dreamscapes of Surrealism in an accompanying commentary entitled *Xunqin's dream*. He notes that:

> He generally utilises the dream as a method of observation and wants to extract some metaphysical elements from reality. He dreams, thinks and appreciates, and wants to seize this incredible state of mind. His dreams express his flowing, surreal heart! This heady dream, with layers of interrelationships, will never end until the end of his life, when he can no longer create. Since Xunqin's dream is distanced from reality, he can't fully address the era in which we live. However, in a surreal dream, there should also be elements of realism, and a reflection on the present day.[39]

Fu Lei's description of Pang Xunqin's artistic processes as surreal very much chimes with André Breton's own definition of Surrealism as 'psychic automatism', but combined with a sense of social awareness and revolutionary fervour of the present day that the Parisian Surrealists would develop from 1925 onwards with the publication of *La Révolution Surréaliste* where anti-colonial and anti-nationalist sentiments were expressed reaching their apogee with the pamphlet 'Ne Visitez pas L'exposition Coloniale' [Don't Visit the Colonial Exhibition] in 1931.[40] We can intuit both an

39. Fu Lei, 'Xunqin de meng' [Xunqin's dream], *Yishu Xunkan* 3 (1932): 15–16.
40. The colonial exhibition that the Surrealists protested against were a form of World's Fair, mounted to bolster public pride in European countries' imperial presence around the world. These events were highly popular and attended by millions of ordinary people in the West. Displays included highly racist

aesthetic and a social awareness of Surrealism when dissecting the symbolism of *Such Is Paris* and *Such Is Shanghai*.

Pang's relationship with Surrealism deepened further when he created the front cover for literary Francophile Fu Lei's Chinese translation of Phillipe Soupault's work *Charlot* (1931), which detailed the life of Hollywood star Charlie Chaplin. Pang would also create other works commissioned as advertisements during the 1930s for items such as cigarettes and Houbigant perfume. The ability of incongruous juxtapositions to halt the eye alongside the intrigue of the dreamscape precipitated many Surrealist commissions for commercial work, particularly advertisements. Indeed, Man Ray's photographs first appeared in French *Vogue* in 1924.[41] Moreover, Surrealism lends itself to advertising due to its inherent focus on subconscious desire,[42] something that was readily translatable into the commercial hub of Shanghai. Soupault was deeply involved in the French Surrealist movement having written the first ever Surrealist novel *Les Champs Magnétiques* [Electric fields] with André Breton in 1919. Alongside renowned philosophers such as Kant and Hegel, the Surrealists admired Charlie Chaplin for his comedy of the everyday and their ideal of automatism, which they believed his physical, slapstick brand of comedy embodied. Here, Pang elaborates Chaplin with reductive,

---

'Human zoos', where non-Western individuals were used as living exhibits and often mistreated by crowds that gathered around them. These displays were intended to emphasize the so-called 'primitive' characteristics of non-Western peoples versus supposed European 'civilisation'; again this acted as a form of justification for colonialism's economic exploitation.

41. Several works of Surrealist photo-literature, such as Andre Breton's *Nadja* (1928), contain advertisements.

42. Kate Nettleton, Robert Saville, and Paul Burke, 'Advertising . . . Surrealism . . . Iguanas', *Campaign* 29, no. 3 (2009): 22.

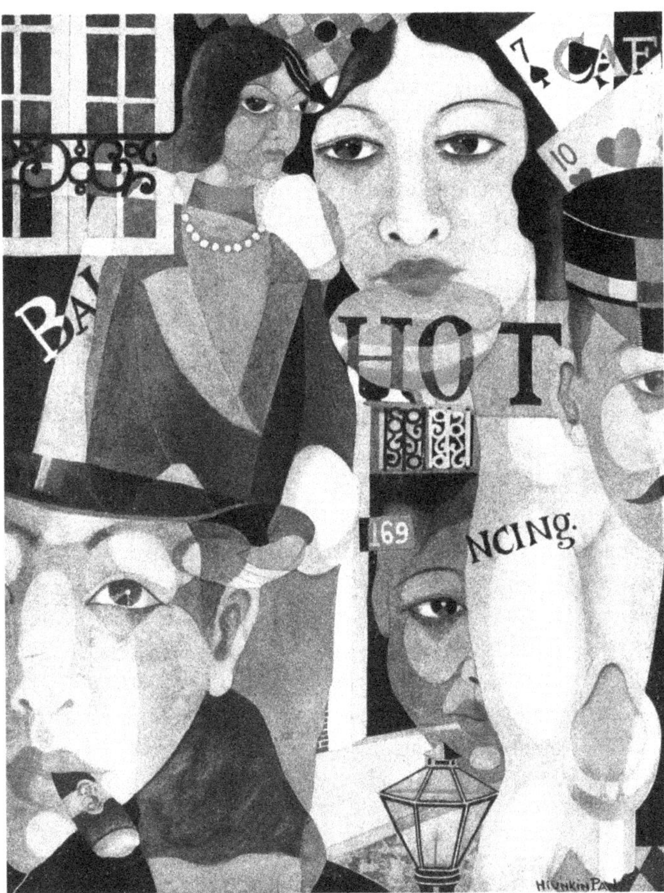

Figure 6. Pang Xunqin (1931), *Such Is Paris* (watercolour on paper). Lost in 1937. Courtesy of Pang Hiunkin (Pang Xunqin) Archives at the Li Ching Cultural and Educational Foundation.

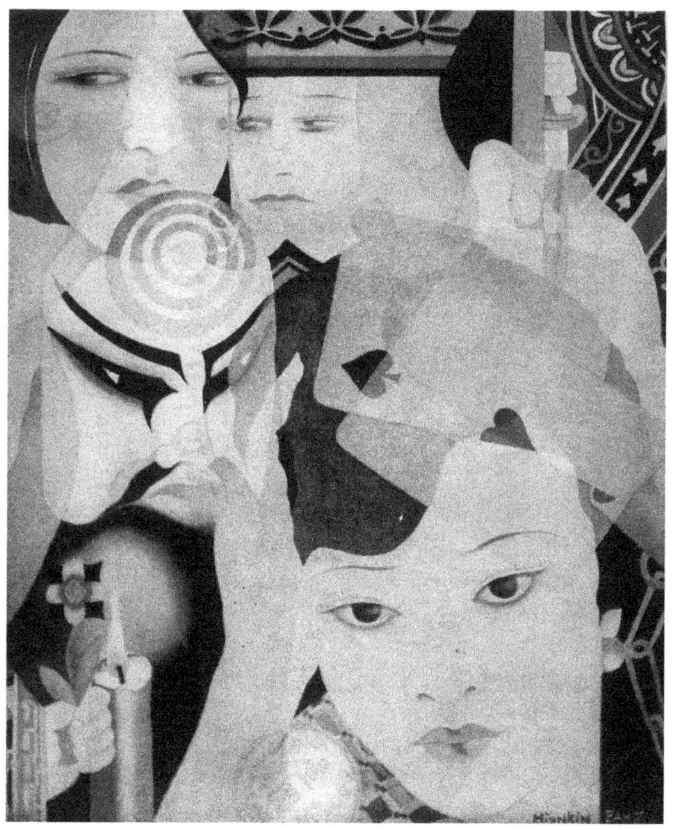

Figure 7. Pang Xunqin (1932), *Such Is Shanghai* (watercolour on paper). Lost in 1937. Courtesy of Pang Hiunkin (Pang Xunqin) Archives at the Li Ching Cultural and Educational Foundation.

exaggerated features for advertising appeal. Fu Lei's translation of Soupault's novel appeared in Ni Yide's *Yishu Xunkan* over multiple instalments, making the magazine a key disseminator of both Surrealist aesthetics and French literature in Shanghai.

Pang Xunqin's artwork was displayed at all four exhibitions of the Storm Society held at various locations in Shanghai's French Concession between 1932 and 1935. Arguably Pang's most Surrealistic work is also fraught with the most incisive social commentary. At the fourth and final exhibition of the Storm Society, Pang exhibited an untitled composition tinged by Marxist undertones. Pang gives his own interpretation of the work in his autobiography: 'The robot symbolises the advanced industrialisation of capitalist countries, the peasant woman represents the defunct agricultural movement in China whilst the three fingers represent the three scourges of imperialism, reactionary politics and feudalism.'[43] This constitutes a potent synthesis of all the political tensions accruing in 1930s China within the space of one canvas. Granted the acuity of the political situation in China, a Surrealist allegory provided a means to escape censorship.

Iconographically speaking, we can clearly distinguish a sky scattered with clouds, disembodied heads, obscure machinery and incongruous juxtapositions, in such a way that several characteristics of Surrealist painting synthetically manifest themselves. This work constitutes the apotheosis of Pang's new-found hybridity in that it cannot be classed as either Chinese or European. As French historian Gruzinski notes 'The hybrid dethrones the exotic, a new manner, at

43. Pang, *Jiushi zheyang zouguolaide*, 142.

least a variant on old European cosmopolitanism, to distance oneself from our place of origin and distinguish oneself from the rest of the population.'[44] In effect, Pang undermines the exotic perception of China by the West, avoiding cultural clichés through deploying Western iconography to tackle Chinese socio-political issues.

As total war broke out with Japan in 1937, it became clear that Surrealism was not an approach Pang could continue with in the midst of conflict. Pang fled Shanghai's French Concession to seek solace in the south-western city of Kunming where he sympathetically depicted the rural idylls of China's ethnic minorities, a stark contrast to his hybrid and often subversive, Surrealist visions of Shanghai and Paris. Instead of assimilating into the norms of Western modernism, as Pang felt compelled to do in Paris, he instead felt compelled to self-censor via rural tropes. Hence, Pang's unique form of Chinese Surrealism could only flourish within a small window of relative freedom in the cosmopolitan milieu of Shanghai's French Concession. Pang's Surrealist activity undoubtedly peaked as a member of the Storm Society, buoyed by fellow artists whom the movement had also influenced. Hence, the society itself and the extent to which Surrealism infiltrated its pioneering cohort is worthy of further analysis.

44. Serge Gruzinski, *La Pensée métissée* (Paris: Fayard, 2012), 2.

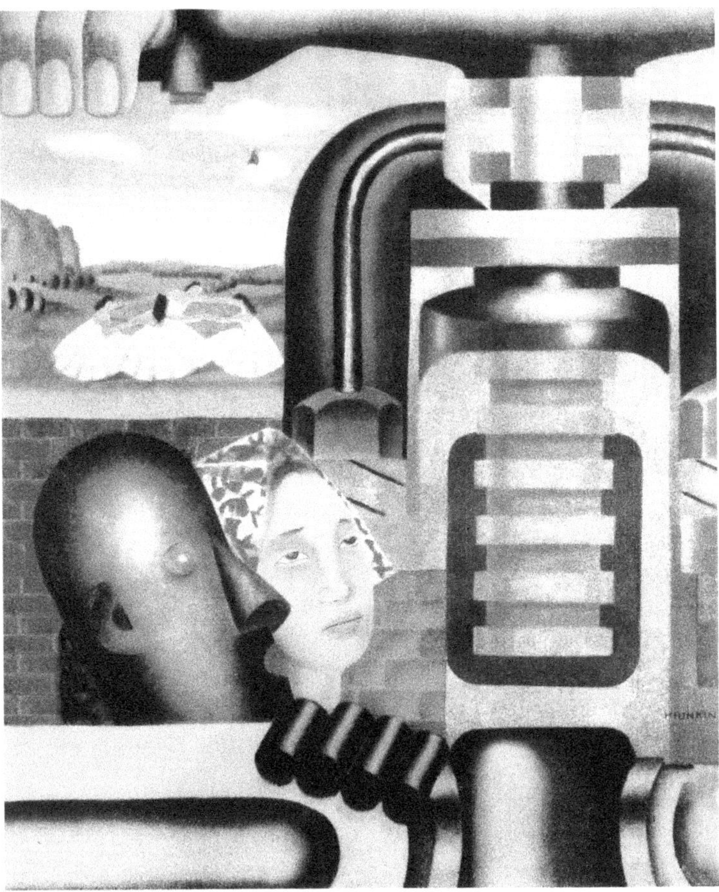

Figure 8. Pang Xunqin (1935), *Untitled* (oil on canvas). Work destroyed in 1966, available as front cover of *Duli Manhua* [Oriental puck] 4 (October 1935). Courtesy of Pang Hiunkin (Pang Xunqin) Archives at the Li Ching Cultural and Educational Foundation.

THE STORM SOCIETY

The Storm Society was founded in 1932 by Pang Xunqin and Ni Yide. As previously noted, the pair had become acquainted while teaching at the Shanghai Art College and brought together several artists who had returned from abroad and/or trained in Western styles. The Shanghai Art College, also located in the French Concession, was partly supported by French government funding and offered courses in Western art. It is where many Storm Society members studied and taught.[1] In their ephemeral lifespan, the Storm Society held four exhibitions in Shanghai's French Concession while their paintings were reproduced in copious periodicals, largely based within the Concession's boundaries.

The Storm Society contributed to a tangible Surrealist aesthetic that permeated Shanghai's cultural landscape during the 1930s. This was underpinned by the blossoming print culture of the French Concession, reproductions of works manifesting clear Surrealist influences abounding in numerous periodicals. However, drawing from Walter Benjamin's seminal terminology regarding the 'aura' of an

1. Jane Zheng, *The Modernization of Chinese Art: The Shanghai Art College, 1913–1937* (Leuven: Leuven University Press, 2016), 134.

original artwork,[2] direct engagement with Surrealist paintings in an exhibition context was limited to a select group of art aficionados. Exhibitions did not make Shanghai the centre of the Chinese art world – rather publishing houses and periodicals became the primary method of cultural engagement – the exhibition simply serving as a catalyst for a pictorial spread in widely disseminated publications. Consequently, the importance of an original artwork's aura exponentially decreased. The circulation of photographs catalysed by Shanghainese print culture also enabled a mediated contact with different iconographies, which could give rise to a hybrid artistic style such as that encouraged by the Storm Society.

For example, the journal *Yishu Xunkan* (1932–1933), which also bore the French title *L'Art*, edited by Ni Yide was thus a principal organ to disseminate the Storm Society's activities. The manifesto of the Storm Society was first published in *Yishu Xunkan* on 11 October 1932, to coincide with their first exhibition (held from 9–16 October 1932) at 'The China Society for the Study of the Arts (*Zhonghua Xueyishe*) on Route Victor Emmanuel III (now Shaoxing Road) in the French Concession'.[3] Ralph Crozier notes the mitigating factors impacting on the first exhibition: 'Because of limited finances, they could only afford the reception hall of the Chinese Art Students' Society which was rather poorly located for drawing the attention of the general public and

2. See Walter Benjamin and James Amery Underwood, *The Work of Art in the Age of Mechanical Reproduction* (London: Penguin Books, 2008).
3. Julia Andrews and Kuiyi Shen, *The Art of Modern China* (Berkeley: University of California Press, 2012), 77.

had inadequate light for showing the paintings.'[4] Despite these setbacks, the exhibition garnered several positive reviews. In particular, the most popular daily newspaper at the time, *Shenbao* [Shanghai News], wrote favourably of the exhibition commenting on 10 October 1932: 'Whilst there are not many works on display at this exhibition, a fresh atmosphere prevails.'[5] Indeed, the Storm Society were certainly the first modernist group in China to empirically utilise elements of Surrealism and other modernist currents and this was a watershed moment with an enduring legacy, despite the limited appeal the exhibition held at time.

Ni Yide's *Yishu Xunkan* published a black and white spread of nine paintings included within the first exhibition of the society.[6] The majority of these were relatively sedate portraits and landscapes painted in a Post-Impressionist style, unlikely to shock more conservative tastes. However, two works manifested nascent elements of Surrealism. In particular, Yang Taiyang, a student of Western painting at the Shanghai Art College, displayed *Two Nude Women*, which comprises contiguous, essentialised figures comporting ethereal stares into the distance. The foregrounded woman holds the sempiternal symbol of eroticism, a bunch of grapes. Further to this, Shanghai Art College graduate and teacher Zhang Xian's *Still Life* appears as a self-referential work celebrating Parisian culture (besides Pang Xunqin he

4. Ralph Crozier, 'Post-Impressionism in Pre-war Shanghai: The Juelanshe (Storm Society) and the Fate of Modernism in Republican China', in *Modernity in Asian Art*, ed. John Clark 1993 (Broadway, NSW, Australia: Wild Peony, 1993), 135–54.
5. Changshu Art, 2004 'Haishang Juelan' [The Storm Society at Sea], accessed 24 July 2020, http://www.changshuart.com/content/article.asp?typeid=34&id=327&keyword=庞薰琹.
6. *Yishu Xunkan* 1, no. 12 (1932): 11.

was the other member of the Storm Society to have studied abroad in Paris) with a French-language art journal replete with sketches, offset by a bottle of wine. Indeed, newspaper fragments were a feature of Surrealist collages and novellas, while also being used by other modernist currents such as Dadaism and Cubism – Picasso's early works being a prominent example of the latter trend.

Although not included in the *Yishu Xunkan* spread, perhaps one of the most overtly Surrealist entries to the first Storm Society exhibition has simply never been reproduced. According to the cartoonist Ye Qianyu, Liang Baibo, one of two female Storm Society members,[7] exhibited an oil painting that was comprised of 'a headless and armless female body',[8] a clear linkage to Surrealist iconography that manipulated the female form in an expression of what the Surrealists termed 'convulsive beauty', whereby 'Beauty, far from reassuring the onlooker, is disclosed as violent and unexpected.'[9] Ye Qianyu somewhat dubiously states: 'If you are a pragmatic pleasure-seeker, then doesn't the most sensual part of the female body reside in the breast down to the thigh?', praising Liang for her insight into the female form in comparison to male artists.[10] As there is no visual record

7. The other female member of the Storm Society was the wife of Pang Xunqin, Qiu Ti. A consummate painter in her own right, she worked in a Post-Impressionist idiom and is not analysed here solely due to the remit of her artistic practice not aligning with Surrealism.
8. Peng Hu, 'Duomian numanhuajia: Liang Baibo de huihua shijie' [A multi-faceted female cartoonist: Liang Baibo's world of painting], *Mei yu shidai* [Modern aesthetics] 4 (2011): 72–77.
9. Krzysztof Fijalkowski and Michael Richardson, *Surrealism: Key Concepts* (New York: Routledge, 2016), 186.
10. Peng Hu, 'Duomian numanhuajia: Liang Baibo de huihua shijie' [A multi-faceted female cartoonist: Liang Baibo's world of painting], *Mei yu shidai* [Modern aesthetics] 4 (2011): 72–77.

of Liang's entry to the First Storm Society Exhibition, we can only speculate as to her artistic impetus for this particular piece. Yet, locating this lost work within her wider artistic practice of the period, one wonders whether Liang's work rather merits a positioning in the realm of parody.

One untitled work particularly stands out in this regard and has been synthesised by art historian Wangwright as 'a Surrealistic image of a tiny man balanced on top of a giant upright key, his arms and legs thrown wide in his excitement over a massive, disembodied leg of a woman'.[11] This work, published in 1936 in *Shanghai Manhua* [Shanghai sketch], a publication featuring 'a mixture of drawings and photographs, with the pictorial inventory ranging from advertisements to social criticism to political'.[12] As such, Liang infantilises and ridicules fetishist tendencies, the male's intact body is metamorphosed into minutiae whilst a hyperbolised and magnified object of desire overwhelms his miniscule stature. Within the periodical issue as a whole, Liang's work is framed against portends of impending conflict with Japan, harbingers of doom offset against the satiation of individual desire which appears to transcend the urgency of the overarching social context.

In 1933, a spread of the Second Storm Society Exhibition was included in the most popular pictorial of the era *Liangyou Huabao*, known in English as *The Young Companion*. During the 1930s the circulation of this magazine

---

11. Amanda Wangwright, *The Golden Key: Modern Women Artists and Gender Negotiations in Republican China (1911–1949)* (Leiden: Brill, 2021).
12. Ellen Johnston Laing, 'Shanghai Manhua: The Neo-Sensationist School of Literature, and Scenes of Urban Life', Modern Chinese Literature and Culture Resource Centre Publication, 2020. https://u.osu.edu/mclc/online-series/shanghai-manhua/.

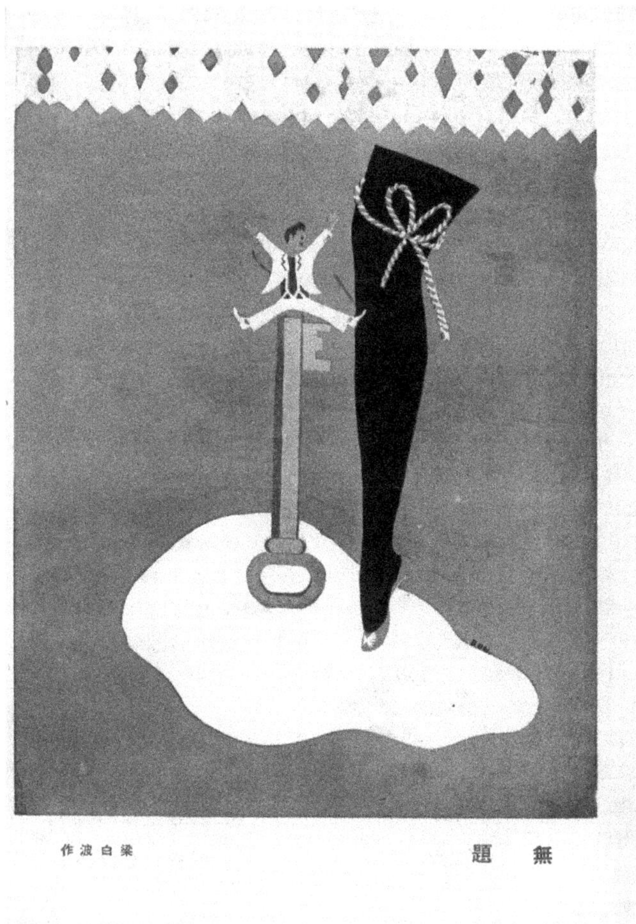

Figure 9. Liang Baibo (1936), *Untitled*, in *Shanghai Manhua* [Shanghai sketch] 3 (1936): 15. Image courtesy of Shanghai Library.

averaged 40,000 copies per issue.[13] The second exhibition was held at the Fukaisen Road[14] World Hall in the French Concession, and opened that October. In his autobiography, Pang Xunqin comments that this exhibition was attended by fewer visitors than the first, however, the real success was that several paintings from the exhibition were reproduced in both *Liangyou* and its competitor *Shidai Huabao* [Modern miscellany].

At this exhibition, copious works demonstrated particularly Surrealist qualities. Indeed, Crozier singles out 'the Surrealistic still lives of Zhou Duo and Yang Taiyang'.[15] In particular, *Still Life* by Yang Taiyang commingles Magritte's cloudscapes and his infamous pipe with a Greco-Roman head reminiscent of Giorgio de Chirico, a synthesis of Surrealism's repertoire of iconic symbols. Another of Yang Taiyang's paintings from this exhibition was reproduced in *Shidai Huabao*, entitled *Chimney and Mandolin*.[16] Yang's work clearly references Picasso's copious deformations of this Western instrument, which is set atop some form of power station, utilising the Surrealist technique of incongruous juxtaposition to suffuse incompatible elements of reality together in order to create a dreamscape. By inserting two

13. Chuchu Wang, 'Distributing Liangyou', in *Liangyou: Kaleidoscopic Modernity and the Shanghai Global Metropolis, 1926–1945*, ed. Paul G. Pickowicz, Kuiyi Shen, and Yingjin Zhang (Leiden: Brill, 2013), 248.
14. Fukaisen Road is a transliteration of Route Ferguson or Ferguson Road, named after the American educator John Calvin Ferguson, who originally built the road to improve access to the Nanyang Public School where he worked. After the founding of the People's Republic of China, the name was changed to Wukang Lu.
15. Crozier, 'Post-Impressionism in Pre-war Shanghai', 146.
16. Xiao Wang, *Ershi Shiji Zhongguo Xihua Wenxian Juelanshe* [Twentieth-century Western-style painting in China: The Storm Society] (Beijing: Wenhua yishu chubanshe, 2004), 203.

pears into the composition, Yang is ostensibly parodying the classical genre of the still life, contorting it to actual elements of Shanghainese everyday existence such as rampant industrialisation embodied by the factory.

In an interview with the Zheng Shengtian, an artist who grew up in Mao's China before emigrating to Canada, Yang Taiyang notes that he did not study abroad before engaging with the Storm Society but instead voraciously read periodicals and books that reproduced works of Western art, affirming the indispensable impact of print culture upon artistic creation in Shanghai.[17] In this same interview, Yang Taiyang very much couches Lu Xun's concept of 'grabbism' as the modus operandi of the society noting:

> By mastering new things from other nations, we understood that we should learn from the advancements of other nations, that we should borrow from their art, and that once we had a grasp of these things, we should learn to use them as tools and to take them further with our own strengths. That was the direction we were going.[18]

Despite this affirmation, it is hard to distinguish any specifically Chinese traits in Yang Taiyang's two paintings here. Indeed, Yang appears to reside in the phase of assimilation Pang Xunqin passed through in Paris. The hybrid commingling of Chinese and Western iconography of Pang Xunqin's work during his affiliation with the Storm Society is not visible in Yang's. However, what is certain is that Yang

17. From 1935, after the Storm Society disbanded, until 1937 (before the outbreak of the Sino-Japanese War) Yang Taiyang did decide to go to Japan to study art.
18. Sheng Project, 'Yang Taiyang and the Storm Society' (2016), http://sheng-project.com/curatorial-projects/shanghai-modern/shanghai-modern-texts/yang-taiyang-and-the-storm.html.

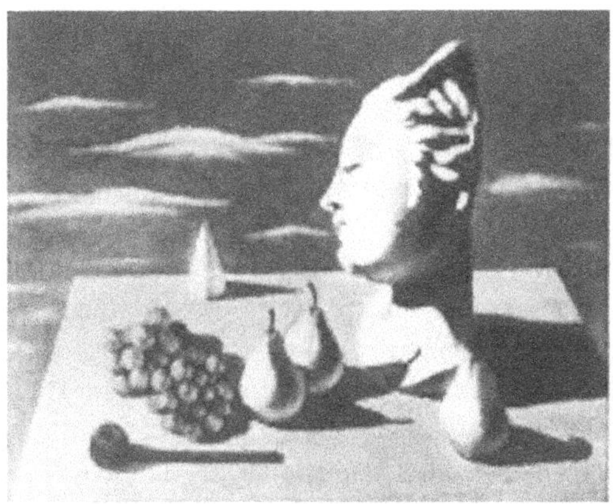

Figure 10. Yang Taiyang (1933), *Still Life*, in *Liangyou Huabao* 82 (1933): 30. Image courtesy of Shanghai Library.

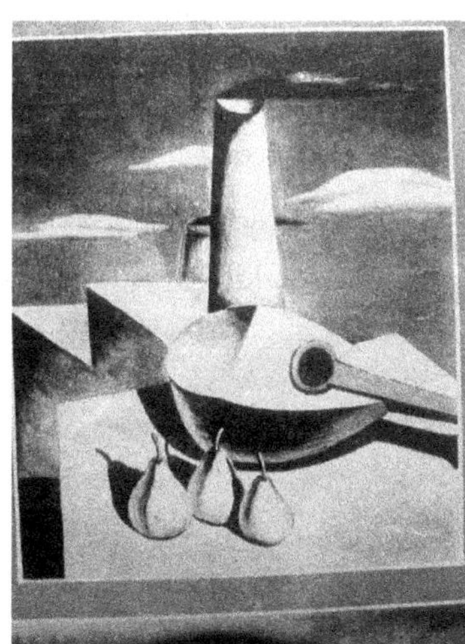

Figure 11. Yang Taiyang (1933), *Chimney and Mandolin*. Courtesy of Tao Yongbai and Asia Art Archive.

is not merely copying Western Surrealist works but rather extracting Surrealist iconography and techniques to create his own highly original dreamscapes with a somewhat ludic, non-threatening intent, bereft of some of the darker aspect of many of his European counterparts in spite of the turbulent social context that pervaded 1930s Shanghai.

A work by Zhou Duo entitled *Odds and Ends* in English but *Untitled* in Chinese appears to incorporate elements of Surrealist assemblage especially reminiscent of the Paris-based Surrealists' gathering of objects from flea market stalls as an affront to high art. This is something that comes to the fore in Breton's *Nadja* and is also present in the review *La Révolution Surréaliste*, texts that are cited in Shanghainese periodicals of the same time period. A familiarity with Marcel Duchamp's concept of the ready-made was also apparent from Pang Xunqin's *Such Is Paris*. Lehmann, a cultural historian, helpfully defines Surrealist assemblage as: 'fostered by the encounter of heterogeneous objects, either through a ludic process of chance or concrete artistic composition'.[19]

Zhou Duo seems to be working in the latter idiom, taking mundane objects, haphazardly scattered on a desk, a hybrid mixture of traditional Chinese and Western elements which constitute a microcosm of Shanghainese everyday life at the time. Zhou Duo eventually gained access to study abroad in Japan after his application was supported by the Shanghai Art College in 1933.[20] Beyond works exhibited in the Storm

19. Ulrich Lehmann, 'Assimilation Objects; Commodities; Fashion', in *A Companion to Dada and Surrealism*, ed. David Hopkins (Chichester: Wiley-Blackwell, 2016), 431.
20. J. Zheng, 'A New Ladder Leading to Celebrity: The Shanghai Art School and the Modern Mechanism of Artistic Celebrity (1913–1937)', *Art Criticism* 22 (2007): 7–28, 10.

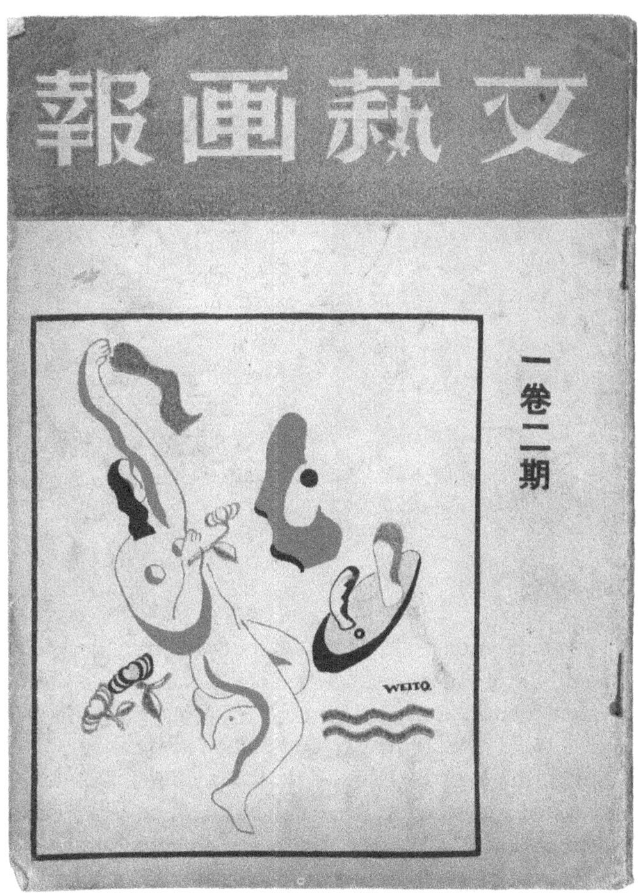

Figure 12. Zhou Duo (1934), Cover design for *Wenyi Huabao* 1, no. 2, in Paul Bevan, *Intoxicating Shanghai: An Urban Montage: Art and Literature in Pictorial Magazines during Shanghai's Jazz Age* (Leiden: Brill, 2020), 63. Photograph courtesy of Paul Bevan.

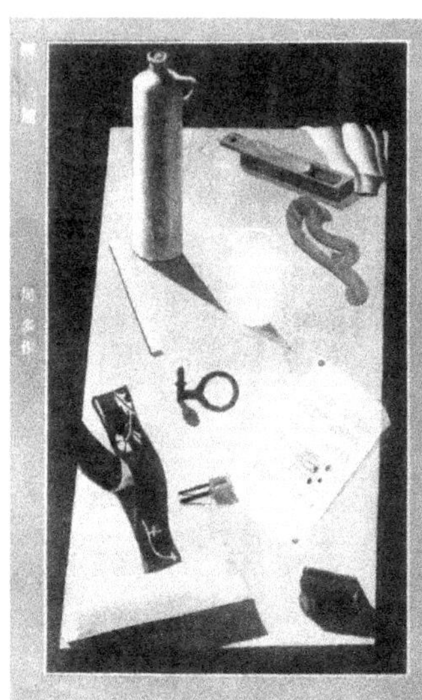

Figure 13. Zhou Duo (1933), *Untitled*, in *Shidai Huabao* [Modern miscellany] 5, no. 1 (1933). Image courtesy of the Shanghai Library.

Society exhibition itself, Zhou Duo produced front covers for the periodical *Wenyi*, which Paul Bevan has revealed to be a hitherto unacknowledged source of Surrealism in China.[21] Zhou's front cover for the second edition of the magazine is clearly inspired by Picasso's Surrealist period, incorporating rounded shapes of a distorted and essentialised female nude holding a flower, surrounded by several abstract forms.

The third exhibition of the Storm Society was held in October 1934 at the French Study Abroad Association

21. Paul Bevan, *'Intoxicating Shanghai'—An Urban Montage: Art and Literature in Pictorial Magazines during Shanghai's Jazz Age* (Leiden: Brill, 2020), 66–67.

on Shipu Road.[22] Pang Xunqin notes that this exhibition boasted the greatest attendance.[23] Paintings from the exhibition were reproduced in the journal *Dazhong Huabao* [The cosmopolitan]. Here, the society became more daring, both aesthetically and politically when compared with their rather demure offerings at the first exhibition. In *Dazhong Huabao*, two nudes are juxtaposed on the journal spread. Yang Taiyang's nude, simply entitled *Renti* [Human figure], directly confronts the viewer in a highly sexualised pose complete with drapery and starkly delineated contours separating the human form from its surroundings. In another text, Yang's piece is called *Haibian Luonu*, which means 'Seaside Nude', confirming the backdrop of this black and white reproduction.[24] Duan Pingyou's nude is presented in a more romanticised modality, sojourning against a scenic backdrop, the head knowingly rotated away from the viewer's scopophilic gaze, the brushstrokes of the body attuned to those of the landscape in the background. The third exhibition of the Storm Society almost treated the inclusion of the nude as a commonplace trope within an avant-garde exhibition, despite the inherent incompatibility of the nude with Chinese traditional culture.

While this academic, heavily studied style of nude is not something the Surrealists approved of, in a Chinese context, this was certainly a complete break from any lingering vestiges of national painting. Ironically, Storm Society member Ni Yide called for the revitalisation of the landscape

22. During the time of the French Concession, Shipu Road was officially called Rue Bourgeat. The name was later changed to Changle Lu.
23. Pang Xunqin, *Jiushi zheyang zouguolaide* (Beijing: Shenghuo, dushu, xinzhi sanlian shudian, 2005), 143.
24. Xiao, *Ershi Shiji Zhongguo Xihua Wenxian Juelanshe*, 199.

genre in order to regain a form of 'national spirit'. However, offsetting a traditional landscape with nudes was perhaps not what he had in mind.[25] Moreover, in *Dazhong Huabao*, as in the exhibition itself, these two nudes were juxtaposed with Pang Xunqin's *Son of the Earth* (1934). The title of the spread as a whole was simply called *Renti* or human form. *Son of the Earth* was a highly politicised artwork depicting a dead boy slumped in his parents' arms in a pieta-like composition,[26] victims of flooding with no support from authorities. Pang recollects that after this piece was displayed in the third Storm Society exhibition, he received death threats due to the subject matter of the work. Fellow Storm Society member Zhang Xian also called him up to warn him the police were on their way to arrest him. As such, Pang temporarily fled to the international concession until he ascertained the threat had passed.[27] Although these works on their own do not indicate intrinsic Surrealist qualities, it is through their shocking juxtaposition as a periodical spread that they acquire a Surrealist status, emphasising the inequality between middle-class erotic desire and the political and financial hardship of the peasant class. Such incongruous juxtapositions in periodicals appear particularly reminiscent of George Bataille's *Documents* (1929–1930), where erotic and macabre images were placed side by side.

The fourth and final exhibition of the Storm Society was held in October 1935 at the same location as the first, the China Society for the Study of the Arts. Works were

---

25. Zheng, *The Modernization of Chinese Art*, 232.
26. Xiaoqing Zhu, 'Pang Xunqin (1906–1985): A Chinese Avant-Garde's Metamorphosis, 1925–1946, and Questions of "Authenticity"' (PhD thesis, University of Maryland, 2009), 103.
27. Pang, *Jiushi zheyang zouguolaide*, 141.

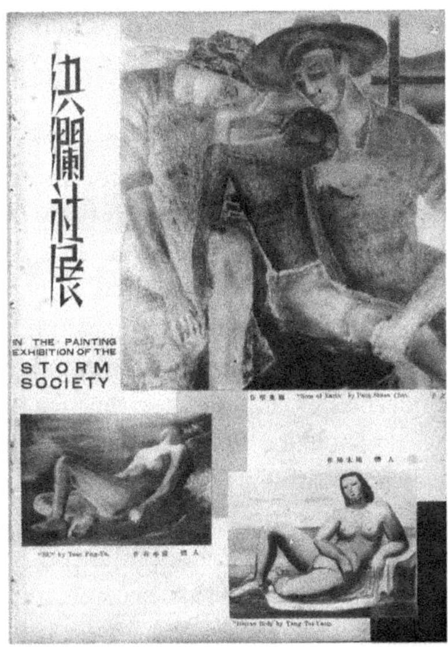

Figure 14. Exhibition of the Storm Society (1934), *Dazhong Huabao* [The cosmopolitan] 12 (1934): 15. Courtesy of Pang Hiunkin (Pang Xunqin) Archives at the Li Ching Cultural and Educational Foundation.

subsequently republished in *Liangyou Huabao* in November 1935.[28] Due to a typo, the fourth exhibition is actually labelled as the third exhibition, causing some confusion. The spread is positioned alongside the Shanghai exhibition of the Chinese Independent Art Association in order to align the artistic endeavour of both avant-garde groups. The standout work from this final exhibition is undoubtedly Pang Xunqin's Surrealist composition juxtaposing a peasant woman's head with a robot, which was explored in the previous case study of the artist. In his autobiography, Pang Xunqin observed that very few people made it to the exhibition and at this

28. *Liangyou Huabao* 111 (November 1935): 21.

point the society disbanded.[29] Notwithstanding, the art critic Sun Fuxi regarded the exhibition as a maturing of the Storm Society's art practice.[30]

Apart from the commercial failure of the final exhibition, other factors came into play. Chinese art historian Xu Kan notes that the Storm Society was not a unified body of painters,[31] with many artists pursuing different currents of modernism, certain members only having a shallow understanding of the movements they were borrowing from.[32] While Ni Yide, for example, had a highly in-depth knowledge of Surrealism, he was concerned as an educator that many of the Storm Society's work could be perceived as having been copied, and therefore advocated a return to the landscape genre, albeit utilising Western techniques. Admittedly, Surrealism formed just one of those countervailing forms of influence upon the Storm Society, but one that became very prominent.

By 1935, war with Japan was becoming an increasingly inevitable prospect, which in turn reinvigorated a drive towards patriotic art that the often hybrid, psychologically orientated creations of the Storm Society did not adhere to. Xu Kan also hints at a competing French and Japanese factions within the Storm Society.[33] What is certain is that while more members of the Storm Society studied in Japan than in France, the iconography of the most well-known

29. Pang, *Jiushi zheyang zouguolaide*, 143.
30. Sun Fuxi, 'Juelanshe juxing di si jie zhanlanhui' [The fourth exhibition of the Storm Society], *Yifeng* [Art winds] 3, no. 11 (1935): 60.
31. Arguably, nor was the Parisian Surrealist group and it became increasingly dispersed after the Second World War.
32. Xu Kan, 'Juelanshe weihe jiesan' [Why did the Storm Society disband?] *Meishujie* 11 (2016): 91.
33. Kan, 'Juelanshe weihe jiesan', 91.

European Surrealists is much more visible in their works than those of their Japanese counterparts. The question remains whether that is an issue of social context or artistic preference. The tension between European and Japanese Surrealism was not idiosyncratic to the Storm Society. Next to the spread of the final exhibition of the Storm Society in *Liangyou* were image reproductions of another avant-garde society which had launched an exhibition in Shanghai populated with Surrealist works, The Chinese Independent Art Association. The society's members were students who had returned from study abroad in Japan.

THE CHINESE INDEPENDENT ART ASSOCIATION

The Chinese Independent Art Association (CIAA) was not established in Shanghai, but rather in Japan in 1934 by Chinese artists who were studying there. These artists were mentored by Satomi Katsuzo, a Japanese artist who exhibited at the 1929 Fine Arts exhibition in Shanghai.[1] Indeed, Japan, where Surrealism was already well known by the 1930s, formed another conduit of the movement into China. One of Katsuzo's writings made it into the Shanghai press, translated by the aforementioned Storm Society member Duan Pingyou. In the highly technical article 'Huihua jifa jiangzuo: goutu zhi yanjiu' [A lecture on painting methods: Research on composition], Katsuzo introduces Western pyramidal perspective citing artworks from the Renaissance onwards, the unifying intention of which does not portend to Surrealism's notion of automatism, although it can be intuited in the work of other Western modernists such as Matisse, whom

1. Julia F. Andrews, 'Japanese Oil Paintings in the First Chinese National Fine Arts Exhibition of 1929 and the Development of Asian Modernism', in *The Role of Japan in Modern Chinese Art*, ed. Joshua Fogel (Berkeley: University of California Press, 2012), 204.

Katsuzo cites as an example.[2] As such, I would venture that the Chinese Independent Art Association's penchant for Surrealism was only peripherally linked to Katsuzo and relied more on the fact that 'French Surrealist texts began to be translated and published in various Japanese journals by the late 1920s'.[3] Indeed, the artist Li Dongping, in an article entitled 'Zuixin riben yanghuajie zhanwang' 'Surveying the latest from the world of Western painting in Japan', mentions the translation of Breton's *Surrealism and Painting* into Japanese in 1931.[4] Katsuzo is not cited but rather Japanese Surrealist Fukuzawa Ichiro who Li praises for being directly influenced by French Surrealism.[5] Notwithstanding, Li notes that the Japanese independent art association Ichiro was part of commingled Japanese Surrealism with brutalism and Cubism, stating these works are not 'pure Surrealism'. He somewhat scathingly labels modern Japanese artists as 'the bastards of Surrealism and other isms'.[6] Indeed, likely due to rising tensions with Japan,[7] art historian Wu notes the Chinese Surrealists tended to 'disintermediate their Japanese mentors'.[8]

---

2. Katsuzo Satomi, trans., 'Duan Pingyou 'Huihua jifa jiangzuo: goutu zhi yanjiu' [A lecture on painting methods: Research on composition], *Yishu* [L'Art] 1 (1933): 103–9.
3. Chinghsin Wu, 'Surrealism in Japan', in *The Routledge Companion to Surrealism*, ed. Kirsten Strom (New York: Routledge, 2022), 253.
4. Li Dongping, 'Zuixin riben yanghuajie zhanwang' [Surveying the latest from the world of Western painting in Japan], *Yifeng* [Art winds] 3, no. 2 (1935): 65–67.
5. Li, 'Zuixin riben yanghuajie zhanwang', 65–67.
6. Li, 'Zuixin riben yanghuajie zhanwang', 65–67.
7. Li, 'Zuixin riben yanghuajie zhanwang', 65–67.
8. Chinghsin Wu, 'Reality Within and Without: Surrealism in Japan and China in the Early 1930s', *Review of Japanese Culture and Society* 26 (December 2014): 205.

The CIAA's first show in China was not in Shanghai but in Guangzhou at the Guangzhou Education Centre in March 1935. Looking for greater impact, their second exhibition took place at the same venue of two of the Storm Society's exhibitions in Shanghai, the China Society for the Study of the Arts, in October 1935. Art historian Kuiyi Shen emphasises the popularity of the Shanghai Exhibition and its extensive media coverage with reproductions of works appearing in both *Liangyou* and *Shidai* similarly to the exhibitions of the Storm Society.[9] Yet, in contrast to the Storm Society, who embraced a multitude of modernist currents, the CIAA particularly focused on Surrealism.

Their Shanghai exhibition in October was theoretically offset by a special issue of the periodical *Yifeng* published at the same time, entitled 'Introduction to Surrealism'. Here, core members wrote several articles which combined the work of Chinese Surrealists Zhao Shou and Zeng Ming, alongside their European counterparts including reproductions by Pablo Picasso, Salvador Dalí, Max Ernst, Yves Tanguy, Francis Picabia, André Masson, Joan Miró, Paul Klee, and Giorgio de Chirico in a work totalling 104 pages.

Zhao Shou's piece *Let's Jump*, which featured in the Shanghai exhibition, was considered to be of adequate enough avant-garde credentials to be published in *Liangyou* in November 1935. The very same year, Zhao Shou would translate a concatenated version of Breton's *Manifesto of Surrealism* from Japanese to Chinese for the *Yifeng* special edition on Surrealism, rendering it accessible to a Chinese

---

9. Julia F. Andrews and Kuiyi Shen, *A Century in Crisis: Modernity and Tradition in the Art of Twentieth-Century China* (New York: Guggenheim Museum, 1998), 175.

audience. Selections of the manifesto that Zhao translated seem to particularly focus on three particular facets of Surrealism that gesture towards its psychoanalytic dimensions: desire, madness, and freedom (through the revolution of the mind). Notably, however, the manifesto does not include Breton's own definition of Surrealism as 'psychic automatism' which is a significant omission.[10]

Painters, of course, have always struggled to apply this principle to their work since drawing is a medium more conducive to the free flow of thought, whereas painting requires a more detailed composition. Kuiyi Shen notes that Zhao Shou described Surrealism in the following manner: 'Although so-called Surrealism is "non-realistic" it is not "without reality", it is actually "non-realistic reality".'[11] Zhao Shou's work *Let's Jump* firmly embodies this dialectical precept. Tangible elements of reality are present. Zhao depicts a fish rising up from diverse geometric forms. In Chinese culture, the fish is a symbol of good luck and abundance, hence the image is unambiguously positivist in orientation. Interestingly, in the Surrealist special issue of *Yifeng*, Paul Klee's 1926 work *Around the Fish* is reproduced in black and white, bearing striking iconographic similarities to Zhao Shou's painting, similarly consisting of a fish ensconced in an abundance of geometric shapes.[12] Further to this, one of Zhao Shou's

10. Zhao Shou, trans., 'Chaoxianshizhuyi xuanyan' [Manifesto of Surrealism], *Yifeng* [Art winds] 3, no. 10 (1935): 18–23.
11. Andrews and Shen, *A Century in Crisis*, 175.
12. *Yifeng* [Art winds] 3, no. 10 (1935): 18. This comparison between Klee and Zhao is suggested by Chia-Chiu Tsai, '1930 Niandai dongya chaoxianshi huihua de gong xiang yu shengbien—yi taiwan, zhongguohua hui wei zhu de bijiao kaocha' [The diversification of Surrealistic paintings in East Asia during the 1930s: A study of art associations in Taiwan and China], *Yishuxue Yanjiu* [Art education research] 25 (2019): 130.

fellow CIAA members, Liang Xihong commended Zhao Shou as he had studied André Breton's seminal poetic work of Surrealism *Poisson Soluble* [Soluble fish].[13] *Soluble Fish* was an example of early Surrealist writing which was published at the same time as the *Manifesto of Surrealism* in 1924. Breton explains the principle behind the intriguing phrase in the following way: 'Am I not the soluble fish, I was born under the sign of Pisces, and man is soluble in his thought.'[14] Thus, the offsetting of a fish amongst geometric shapes is no contradiction but merely the merging of two distinct realities as Breton explains via man's recourse towards 'soluble thought', in other words, our subconscious.

According to Wu, Zhao also advocated that Ancient Chinese art contained Surrealist elements. He believed Surrealist painting combined an Eastern spirit with Western techniques.[15] Certainly, many of Zhao Shou's other paintings from this period incorporate thoroughly Chinese iconography that is depicted in a more Western, Surrealist idiom. For example, his work, *Yan* [Face] is in dialogue with the tradition of Chinese opera masks but the figurative shapes are somehow woven into the background and appear as occult-like symbols. The mask was a widely used trope across the spectrum of international Surrealism, often linked to questions of identity which was the source of much tension in a China torn between a feudal hangover, colonial everyday, and war-mongering Japanese aggression.

Beyond Zhao Shou's *Let's Jump*, five other paintings from the CIAA Exhibition in Shanghai were reprinted in

13. Chinghsin Wu, 'Reality Within and Without', 203.
14. André Breton, *Manifestoes of Surrealism*, trans. Richard Seaver and Helen R. Lane (Ann Arbor: University of Michigan Press, 1969), 40.
15. Chinghsin Wu, 'Reality Within and Without', 203.

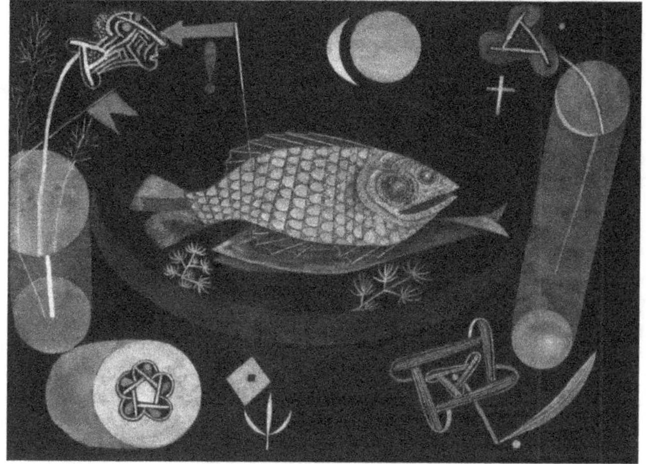

Figure 15. Paul Klee (1926), *Around the Fish* (oil and tempera on canvas mounted on cardboard), 46.7 × 63.8 cm. Courtesy of The Museum of Modern Art, New York/Scala, Florence.

Liangyou on the following page from the final exhibition of the Storm Society.[16] Art historian Chia-Chiu Tsai convincingly argues that *Desire* by Bai Sha was adapted from Salvador Dalí's *The Accommodations of Desire*, created in 1929. Granted, the faithful translation of the word 'Desire' from the Chinese *Yuwang*, this is a highly plausible line of reception.[17] Dalí superimposed lions' heads onto pebbles,

16. *Liangyou Huabao*, 111 (November 1935): 22.
17. Tsai, '1930 Niandai dongya chaoxianshi huihua de gong xiang yu shengbiena' [The diversification of Surrealistic paintings in East Asia during the 1930s], 130.

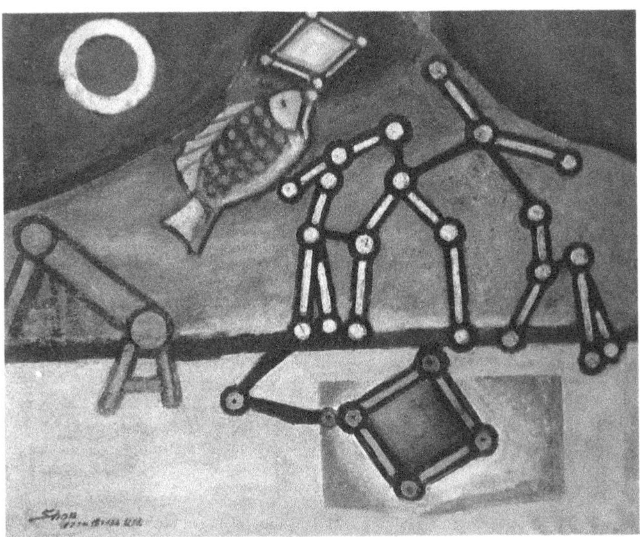

Figure 16. Zhao Shou (1934), *Let's Jump* (oil on canvas), 78 × 93 cm. Guangzhou Art Museum. Published in Julia Frances Andrews and Kuiyi Shen, *A Century in Crisis* (New York: Guggenheim, 1988), 40.

purportedly in an outpouring of sexual frustration underpinned by Freudian psychoanalysis. The black and white nature of Bai Sha's reproduction again impedes detailed analysis, but there does appear to be some form of animal head on one of the pebbles while the other is hollowed out. This work by Dalí was not reproduced in the *Yifeng* special edition, hence it is more likely that Bai Sha could have encountered it during his time in Japan. This direct appropriation of a particular Surrealist painting appears more of an unfinished preparatory study than a work of art in its own right.

Despite this unfettered recourse to the copy, in the *Yifeng* special edition on Surrealism, Bai Sha also published three highly original and authentic Surrealist poems which were entitled in French *Hommage à la peinture surréaliste* [Homage to Surrealist painting], but written in Chinese. This stanza from one of his poems conjured evocative imagery to describe a scene within a Surrealist painting:

Crystal-rose flower,
Within your dangerous veins,
So many great atoms exist.
When the white dog howls towards the sky,
The snail falls from the spire
Within your solid crystals,
It finds a suitable existence.
Feathers are singing on the canvas of Masson,
I avoid the morning glory flower,
If it glows green,
I will watch the world from Notre-Dame cathedral.[18]

André Masson was renowned for his use of natural elements and incorporated feathers into his 1927 composition *Leaf, Feather, Drop of Blood.* As such, Bai Sha clearly intends the poem as an ode to one of the most innovative Surrealist painters vis-à-vis material form.

Another key member and exhibitor at the CIAA was Li Dongping. Li wrote the manifesto of the association which was published in their own journal *Duli Meishu* [Independent art]. Here, in a similar fashion to the Storm Society Manifesto, Li emphasised freedom of creation but also lamented what

18. *Yifeng* [Art winds] Volume 3, Issue 10 (1935): 48.

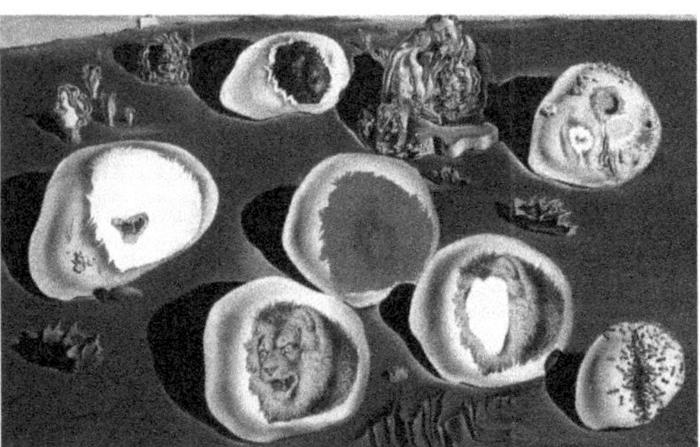

Figure 17. Salvador Dalí (1929), *The Accommodation of Desires* (oil and cut-pasted printed paper on wood), 22.2 × 34.9 cm. The Metropolitan Museum of Art New York. © Salvador Dalí, Fundació Gala-Salvador Dalí, DACS 2024.

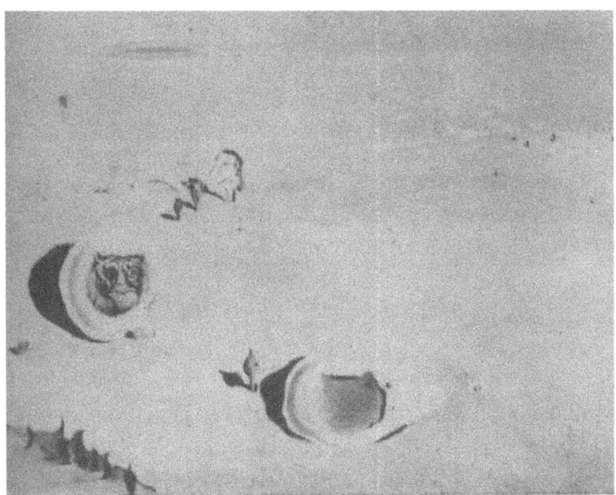

Figure 18. Bai Sha (1935), *Desire* (oil on canvas), in *Liangyou Huabao* 111 (November 1935): 22. Image courtesy of the Shanghai Library.

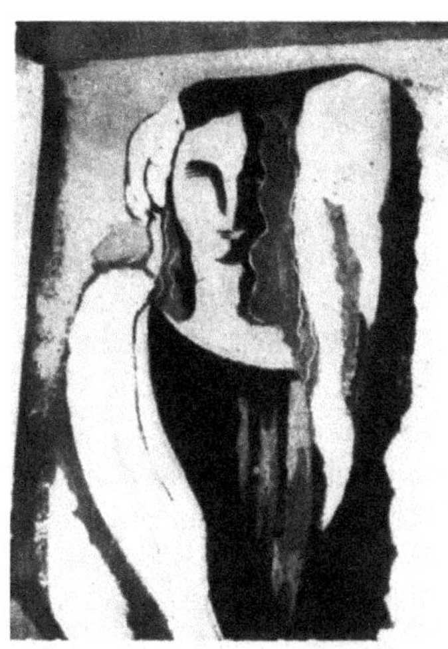

Figure 19. Li Dongping (1935) *After Bathing* in *Yifeng* [Art winds] 3, no. 8 (1935): 30. Image courtesy of the Shanghai Library.

he interprets as China's 'lagging behind' in terms of artistic innovation with the group's near namesake, France's Society of Independent Artists, created over 50 years earlier.[19] His work *After Bathing* was published in the journal *Yifeng* and comprises a highly Picasso-esque work emulating a hand-sculpted, rock-art inspired female in a seductive posture embellished with a compelling use of shadow.

Zeng Ming also presented works at the Shanghai exhibition and wrote for *Yifeng*. In his article 'Chaoxianshizhuyi de shi yu huihua' [Surrealism's poems and paintings] he gave the following explanation of the movement: 'The

19. Li Dongping, 'Zhonghua Duli Meishu Xiehui Xuanyan' [Manifesto of the Chinese Independent Art Association], *Duli Meishu* [Independent art], May 1935. Reproduced in Appendix II.

Surrealist movement is by no means based on traditional artistic concerns, their works do not celebrate anything, instead they are purely working towards one's own internal perception of the world.'[20] As such, we can perhaps intuit that Zeng Ming means that well-known collective phenomena were granted an individual voice and treatment via tapping into the subconscious realm of existence. Indeed, Surrealism was not a style, the First Manifesto noting it was produced beyond aesthetic concerns. His work *Moon Night* (Fig. 20) indeed individualises a genre common in Chinese national painting. The work was also reproduced in the special Surrealist edition of *Yifeng*, possibly drawing from the marvellous aspect of Surrealist thought. Wu describes his work as comprising: 'organic lines and the natural objects, suspended in an undefined space and lit by an indeterminate light source'.[21] The marvellous is a notoriously difficult component of Surrealism to define, however, Surrealist scholar Donna Roberts aptly relates the marvellous to nature commenting, 'André Breton and Louis Aragon both wishing to overcome the divide between man and the natural world, "nature" became a watch-word for the marvellous, the instinctual beneath the civilized, and a historical cipher for uncanny primordial origins.'[22]

Similar teachings are present in Daoist culture, the indigenous religion of China, whereby man is advised to follow nature's rhythm or *Tianren heyi*. Surrealist scholar Noheden highlights a Radio Canada interview 'with Breton

20. *Yifeng* [Art winds] 3, no. 10 (1935): 38.
21. Chinghsin Wu, 'Reality Within and Without', 197.
22. Donna Roberts, 'Surrealism and Natural History: Nature and the Marvelous in Breton and Caillois', in *A Companion to Dada and Surrealism*, ed. David Hopkins (Hoboken, NJ: John Wiley & Sons, 2016), 366.

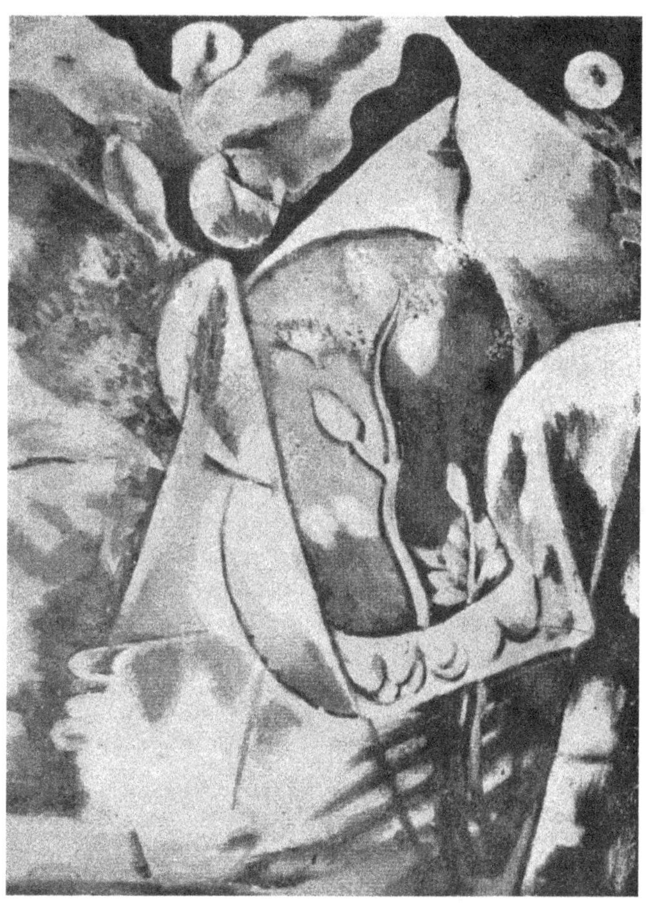

Figure 20. Zeng Ming (1935), *Moon Night* in *Yifeng* [Art winds] 3, no. 10 (1935): 17. Courtesy of the Lyon Municipal Library, collection of the Franco-Chinese Institute of Lyon.

in which alluding to Daoism and alchemy, he called on the need to "follow nature"'.[23] While this interview admittedly took place in 1961, there are clearly resonances between Surrealist and Daoist views that challenge anthropocentrism from the beginnings of the former movement. Indeed, at the 1936 Surrealist Exhibition of Objects at the Galerie Charles Ratton in Paris 'Natural Objects' such as plants and minerals were displayed alongside man-made works.[24] As such, this is a prime example of the marvellous conceived in relation to nature, another Surrealist strand of thought compatible with indigenous Chinese belief systems.

Commenting on the Shanghai exhibition of the CIAA in 1935, art historian Gerwing notes that 'The exhibition in Shanghai which received a theoretical framework by the association's Surrealist manifest aroused massive attention among the progressive intelligentsia of the harbour town', but many spectators were not as taken in by the Surrealist works so no more exhibitions were prepared.[25] Art historian Kao has speculated upon reasons for the group's failure stating: 'Chinese critics were unaware of the revolutionary

---

23. Kristoffer Noheden, 'Toward a Total Animism: Surrealism and Nature', in *The Routledge Companion to Surrealism*, ed. Kirsten Strom (New York: Routledge, 2022), 60.
24. See André Breton, *Exposition d'Objets Surréalistes Chez Charles Ratton* [Exhibition of Surrealist objects at the Charles Ratton Gallery], 1936, available online https://www.andrebreton.fr/en/work/56600100858821?back_url=https%3A%2F%2Fwww.andrebreton.fr%2Fen%2Fview%3Frql%3DRatton%26_fsb%3D1%26subvid%3Dtsearch&back_rql=DISTINCT%20Any%20M%2CMT%2CD%20ORDERBY%20ST%20WHERE%20X%20linked_to%20M%2C%20M%20short_description%20D%2C%20NOT%20X%20identity%20M%2C%20M%20title%20MT%2C%20M%20sorttitle%20ST%2C%20X%20eid%20312973, 3.
25. Jonas Gerwing, *Between Tradition and Modernity – The Influence of Western European and Russian Art on Revolutionary China* (Norderstedt: Books on Demand, 2014).

viewpoints of the Surrealists in Europe . . . they interpreted the subjective involvement in the dreams and fantasies of the Surrealists as an escape from reality, and thus rejected them on such grounds.'[26] It would seem that while Surrealism had an iconographic presence in Chinese art, the movement's political intent was misunderstood. Indeed, the special edition of *Yifeng* magazine dedicated to Surrealism, spearheaded by the CIAA, certainly corroborates Kao's point. No mention is made of the political antecedents to Surrealism such as Hegel, nor of Marx. Only the Freudian aspect is prized by the issue's various writers. Recourse to psychoanalysis and the expression of internal sentiment, nevertheless, constituted a radical disjuncture with the collective values of Confucianism.

Sadly, after the Shanghai exhibition, the CIAA met the same fate as the Storm Society and they gradually disbanded before the outbreak of the Second Sino-Japanese War (1937). There was, however, one highly noteworthy activity after the Shanghai exhibition that should be mentioned. In 1937, in Shanghai-based periodical *Meishu zazhi* [Art magazine], CIAA member Liang Xihong criticised an exhibition by renowned Chinese realist painter Xu Beihong. He comments that Xu Beihong portends to abide by realism, but in fact, his paintings are limited to flowers, *shanshui* [mountain and water] paintings which have very little to do with the real life of ordinary people.[27] He accuses Xu Beihong of imitating the French founder of academic realism Gustave Courbet and not imbuing his own personality into

26. Mayching Margaret Kao, 'China's Response to the West in Art 1898–1937' (PhD diss., University of Stanford, 1975), 195.
27. Liang Xihong, 'Ping Xu Beihong gezhan' [A critique of Xu Beihong's solo exhibition], *Meishu zazhi* [Art magazine] 1, no. 4 (1937): 96–101.

his works.[28] Liang Xiahong believed that Courbet's realism is simply the portrayal of internal feelings on the canvas rather than an accurate depiction of natural phenomenon, something that Xu Beihong had not attained.[29] Interestingly, it would seem that for Liang, the subject matter of *guohua* cannot be reconciled with the Western import of realism and indeed, members of the CIAA, in particular Zeng Ming, were able to align *guohua* with Surrealist ideals unlike artists such as Pang Xunqin of the Storm Society.

Out of all the Surrealist groupings and creations in Shanghai, the CIAA certainly demonstrated the strongest theoretical understanding of the movement, despite their fleeting presence in the city. Paradoxically, such in-depth knowledge about an art movement of European origin was largely garnered in China's neighbouring country of Japan, where Surrealism was a prominent presence from the late 1920s. While there are some instances of direct appropriation rather than engagement, the paintings of the CIAA seem to chime more with Zhao Shou's concept of Surrealism being an Eastern movement in terms of philosophy while drawing from Western aesthetic techniques.

The CIAA works evince a Daoist-like rapport with nature, recourse to traditional Chinese Zodiacal symbology, ancient Chinese culture via Zhao Shou's opera masks, as well as ethereal, figurative renderings of the human form and landscape. Consequently, this somewhat turns Lu Xun's premise of 'grabbism' on its head. Despite the CIAA conspicuously pillaging some well-known Surrealist imagery

28. Liang, 'Ping Xu Beihong gezhan' [A critique of Xu Beihong's solo exhibition], 96–101.
29. Liang, 'Ping Xu Beihong gezhan' [A critique of Xu Beihong's solo exhibition], 96–101.

and techniques, it was actually European Surrealist philosophy that drew from Daoism and traditional Chinese culture as shown in the introduction. In short, Surrealism 'grabbed' a substantial part of its philosophical orientation from the East while members of the CIAA 'grabbed' appealing and provocative Surrealist imagery from the West.

As such, in order to further interrogate the cross-cultural issues at stake in 'Chinese Surrealism', it is necessary to delve deeper into the Chinese reception of prominent Western Surrealists. It was none other than members of the CIAA who wrote on this in the greatest depth.

CHINESE INTERPRETATIONS OF EUROPEAN SURREALIST WORKS

Modern artists in China had mediated contact with European Surrealism via works that were published in the popular periodicals of the day, while a select few had seen such artworks first hand in Paris or on loan to exhibitions in Tokyo. In terms of reproductions in periodicals, the gamut of works referenced by Chinese Surrealists was limited to the most prominent artists of the European movement. In the CIAA's special edition on Surrealism in *Yifeng*, a total of eighteen artists are cited, including two of their own. As Wu notes, no Japanese Surrealists are mentioned, despite the fact that this grouping of Surrealists all studied in Japan and were clearly inspired by their Japanese peers. This is correctly attributed to the mounting tension between the two nations since the colonisation of Manchuria (Northern China) in 1932.[1] Consequently, reproductions of Japanese Surrealist works were very scarce indeed within the pages of Surrealist-leaning Shanghai periodicals.

1. Chinghsin Wu, 'Reality Within and Without: Surrealism in Japan and China in the Early 1930s', *Review of Japanese Culture and Society* 26 (December 2014): 202–203.

The eighteen Surrealist painters were identified in the 1935 *Yifeng* Special edition on the movement were: Pablo Picasso, Giorgio de Chirico, Georges Braque, Carlo Carrà, Joan Miró, André Masson, Yves Tanguy, Man Ray, Max Ernst, André Beaudin, Paul Klee, Hans Arp, Zhao Shou, Z.L. Roux, Pierre Roy, Zeng Ming, Francis Picabia, and Salvador Dalí.[2]

Apart from Zhao Shou and Zeng Ming, both prominent members of the CIAA, this list is limited to a group of European-based male artists who had the most commercial success in the early stages of Surrealism. It does not account for female or non-Western contributions to the movement. Certain inclusions of artists are somewhat questionable, in particular, Carrà was Futurist, Beaudin, Fauvist, Braque, Cubist and some other figures such as Klee, Picasso, and Picabia had more peripheral links to the Surrealist movement. The identity of Z.L Roux is unclear but could point to Gaston Louis Roux whose work resonated with Cubism. This list is perhaps symptomatic of the dual distillation of Surrealism in Shanghai which filtered through Paris and Tokyo before reaching the city's shores. While the fundamentals of the movement had indeed been understood, certain aspects were inevitably lost in translation. It appears then the CIAA had a much more expansive view of what Surrealism was compared to the tight-knit coterie of Bretonian Surrealists in Europe. Certain members of this group had seen European Surrealist art first hand at the Paris-Tokyo Avant-Garde exhibition while studying abroad in Japan.[3]

2. Liang Xihong, 'Chaoxianshizhuyi huajia lun' [Theory of Surrealist painters], *Yifeng* [Art winds] 3, no. 10 (1935): 42.
3. Chinghsin Wu, 'Reality Within and Without', 197.

In terms of reception, traditional Chinese art criticism tends towards conveying the spirituality behind an artwork rather than an appreciation of intricate details. In the sixth century, art critic Xie He elaborated a methodology entitled the 'Six principles of Painting'. The first and most important was 'spiritual resonance' described as 'the energy the artist transmitted in the work'.[4] Spiritual resonance was indeed the impetus behind the creation of Chinese national painting or *guohua*. Within *Yifeng* magazine, rather than an assimilation of European formal analysis, the spirituality of each artwork is teased out. Arguably, many Surrealist works contain spiritual aspects[5] and contrary to popular belief, several notable Surrealists held deep-seated mystical convictions which, in turn, became manifest in their paintings.[6] As such, I would argue that traditional Chinese art criticism unexpectedly complements, to some extent, the analysis of European Surrealist works. Lin Yutang wrote of the founder of the literati school of painting, Su Dongpo (1037–1101) 'the object of drawing is merely to 'express one's mood or

4. For a concise explanation of all six of Xie He's principles please consult Rens Bod, *A New History of the Humanities: The Search for Principles and Patterns from Antiquity to the Present* (Oxford: Oxford University Press, 2015), 49–51. More recently, Craig Clunas has charted the art-historical reception of *qiyun shengdong* in the West with particular attention to its translation. See Craig Clunas, 'Chiang Yee as Art History', in *Chiang Yee and His Circle: Chinese Artistic and Intellectual Life in Britain, 1930–1950*, ed. Paul Bevan, Anne Veronica Witchard, and Da Zheng (Hong Kong: Hong Kong University Press, 2022).
5. These were influenced by Buddhism and borrowings from spirit-deities of African and Oceanian art. Within the Mexican Surrealist group, syncretic elements of Catholicism and indigenous belief systems were another source of inspiration, such as the ritual celebration the Day of the Dead.
6. André Breton himself elaborated a treatise on 'Magic Art' [L'Art Magique] in 1957, which serves as a Surrealist history of art that refutes rationalism, instead contending that all works of art have mystical origins.

feeling' (*hsieh yi*) and the painting need not be a slavish copy of reality. Such work should be done quickly, on the inspiration of the moment.'[7] Lin quotes Su Dongpo's famous statement: "To judge a painting by its verisimilitude shows the mental level of a child".[8]

Western Surrealist painting, through its transgression of reality and spiritual elements, appears to have more in common with the tenets of Chinese art criticism as opposed to the European lineage of formalism and realism. Conversely, European Surrealists were of course, shunned by many conservative art critics during the inter-war years, their international exhibitions sparking off the most negative of diatribes in the press.[9] Perhaps we could go as far as to say that the initial reaction towards Surrealism in China was no less negative than that of the West.

Picasso was resolutely viewed as Surrealist by the CIAA and ostensibly given the most attention of all European Modern Artists. CIAA member Zeng Ming gives a concise history of Picasso's artistic trajectory in the article *Zuijin Bijiasuo de yishu* [Picasso's latest artworks]. He acknowledges his Cubist origins before explaining how André Breton highlighted the Surrealist qualities of his work in the seminal text *Le Surréalisme et la Peinture* [Surrealism and painting].[10] Moreover, throughout the special *Yifeng* edition dedicated

7. Lin Yutang, *The Chinese Theory of Art: Translations from the Masters of Chinese Art* (New York: Putnam Sons), 13.
8. Lin Yutang, *The Chinese Theory of Art: Translations from the Masters of Chinese Art*, 13.
9. For example, the Penrose Collection at the Scottish National Gallery of Modern Art Archive in Edinburgh holds press reaction to the 1936 International Surrealist Exhibition GMA A35/1/1/RPA721.
10. Zeng Ming, 'Zuijin bijiasuo de yishu' [Picasso's latest artworks], *Yifeng* [Art winds] 3, no. 8 (1935): 22–24.

to Surrealism, several of Picasso's preparatory sketches are interspersed within the main body of articles as marginalia. Throughout 1935, *Yifeng* also produced an important series of thirty modern painters within which a specific work and artist were given a dedicated full-page slot comprising the reproduction of an artwork and a paragraph-length critique. This list was compiled by CIAA member Liang Xihong. Liang began his career at the Guangzhou Municipal College of Fine Arts before studying abroad in Japan during 1933 where the CIAA was founded. Returning to China he became well known for writing on various genres of Western art.

While writing on Surrealism, most of his own artworks were more redolent of the Fauvist and Post-Impressionist schools. Unlike Zeng Ming, Liang Xihong categorises Picasso as a Cubist artist but does mention that he also aligned with Surrealism. He also notes that Picasso drew from African art.[11] Moreover, for the special edition of *Yifeng*, Zhao Shou wrote an article entitled in French 'Pablo Picasso et son Rêve de 1929'. In this article he adopts a Surrealist, quasi-poetic tone of writing to describe Picasso's oeuvre, stating: 'his paintings are no more than a geometric circle depicted in the desert, is it mere spectacle? He continues 'his art is like an X-ray'.[12] Perhaps we can extrapolate from these musings that Zhao Shou views Picasso's work as a deeper, spiritual form of reality that requires penetrating beyond the surface of representation.

11. Liang Xihong, 'Xiandai shijie ming huajia: Pablo Picasso' [World-famous modern painters: Pablo Picasso], *Yifeng* [Art winds] 3, no. 2 (1935): 80–83.
12. Zhao Shou, 'Pablo Picasso et son rêve de 1929' [Pablo Picasso and his dream of 1929], *Yifeng* [Art winds] 3, no. 10 (1935): 50.

Further to Picasso, a special one-page article was dedicated to Yves Tanguy. Analysing Tanguy, Liang Xihong states the following in *Yifeng*:

> The Surrealist Tanguy works in a similar style to André Masson, his paintings are filled with the power of rich fantasy, which freely and mysteriously depict the landscape as an ocean. His thought is distanced from reality, and his paintings enact the crystallisation of his thoughts. We can only appreciate his paintings from a dream-like perspective.[13]

Alongside the text, Tanguy's 1927 work *He Did What He Wanted* is reproduced. No direct reference to the accompanying work or its composite elements is made which would be the bread and butter of European formal analysis. Rather, a more fundamental vision of Tanguy's paintings as a mechanism for envisioning his inner-thought process is argued by Liang Xihong.

In a page dedicated to Max Ernst, Liang Xihong notes 'He pursues strange images, believing strangeness is a permanent reality.'[14] This seems to readily equate Ernst's work to Freud's notion of the 'uncanny' whereby something is resoundingly familiar and strange at the same time, again favouring analysis of the underlying spiritual energy behind the painting. This is certainly a valid reading of Ernst's corpus as a whole. However, the work reproduced alongside this text is *Pietà or Revolution by Night* (1923). A pietà denotes a scene wherein Mary is holding the body of Christ

13. Liang Xihong, 'Xiandai shijie ming huajia: Yves Tanguy' [World-famous modern painters: Yves Tanguy], *Yifeng* [Art winds] Volume 3, Issue 12 (1935): 69.
14. Liang Xihong, 'Xiandai shijie ming huajia: Max Ernst' [World-famous modern painters: Max Ernst], *Yifeng* [Art winds] Volume 3, Issue 12 (1935): 71.

after the crucifixion. Ernst reappropriates this scene in an allusion to his troubled relationship with his father who was a strong Catholic and disapproved of his style of painting. This level of contextual detail is not provided for any of the artists in the *Yifeng* magazine.

In another page dedicated to Joan Miró, a work from his *Spanish Dance* series is reproduced. Liang Xihong writes:

> Miró is a lively painter, his painting titles are all lyrical, literary and mysterious. He reveals his passion through his rapid style of painting. He views the world in a poetic manner, depicting moonlight as bright as daylight. His lyrical talent and surreal spirit are as harmonious as music . . . but his paintings incorporate mysterious elements from the real world.[15]

Interestingly, Chinese (or specifically Daoist) notions of harmony are applied to Miró's work. This very much relates to André Breton's aforementioned statement in the *Second Manifesto of Surrealism* that advocates for the reconciliation of opposing forces as a key element of the spirit.[16]

Finally, an article by Liang Xihong on Giorgio de Chirico notes: 'His works can be described as metaphysical . . . His paintings are all incomprehensibly subtle and poetic, combining classical faces and sharp lines.'[17] The spiritual aspect of De Chirico is once again alluded to by framing him as a metaphysical painter but the focus on the line is also a key

15. Liang Xihong, 'Xiandai shijie ming huajia: Juan Miró' [World-famous modern painters: Juan Miró], *Yifeng* Volume 3, Issue 12 (1935): 68.
16. André Breton, *Manifestoes of Surrealism*, trans. Richard Seaver and Helen R. Lane (Ann Arbor: University of Michigan Press, 1969), 123.
17. Liang Xihong, 'Xiandai shijie ming huajia: Giorgio Di Chirico' [World-famous modern painters: Giorgio Di Chirico], *Yifeng* [Art winds] Volume 3, Issue 10 (1935): 91.

element of ancient Chinese art criticism and the second of Xie He's six principles.

The principal critic of Surrealism from the Storm Society was Ni Yide. In a text that preceded the CIAA in 1933, the prominent magazine *Yishu* [L'Art] published an in-depth article on Surrealist painting in Europe in 1933. The writer, Ni Te (a pseudonym for Ni Yide) boldly states, 'Surrealism's cosmopolitan nature extends throughout the world.'[18] This statement is fleshed out by a detailed review of Surrealist painters by countries; citing France, Germany, Italy, and Spain and different tendencies within Surrealism divided into four sub-sets of artist-representatives; namely Pablo Picasso and Georges Braque, Giorgio de Chirico, Joan Miró, and Max Ernst.

Beyond the Storm Society and CIAA, other snippets of Surrealist art criticism did appear in the pages of Shanghai newspapers and periodicals. In July 1936 in the *China Pictorial* (*Zhonghua*) a cartoon was used to lampoon the thought processes behind Surrealist painting, a plant protruding out of the painter's head. Parody of course assumes prior knowledge of a particular movement or trend to be effective so we can therefore deduce that during a highly compressed timeframe, Surrealism in its painterly form had been widely disseminated to the extent that it enjoyed a certain level of popularity throughout the cultural metropolis of Shanghai and in other loci of cultural activity in China. There were, however, overt detractors. Wu Yaozong (also romanised as Y. T. Wu) a protestant Christian who preached a socially engaged, communist-sympathising gospel, wrote an article

18. Ni Te, 'Chaoxianshizhuyi Huihua' [Surrealist painting], *Yishu* [L'Art] Volume 1 (1933): 85–89.

in 1935 entitled 'Qingnian wenti tanzuo: xianshi yu chaoxianshi' [A topic for discussion amongst the youth: Reality and surreality]. Wu notes: 'Some people create illusory castles in the air during these dark times, seeking a spiritual reprieve. This is not the transcendence of reality but rather an escape from reality.'[19] Here, Wu is adopting a politically engaged approach to art, believing it should represent the era it was made in. While Surrealism certainly chimed with the subjectivity of Chinese literati art, it was also a politically charged movement, something this critic either did not seem to be aware of or did not want to state. Although the vast majority of art criticism in the Republican era tended to steer clear of Surrealism's political aspects, one notable exception, however, is the periodical *Xiandai*.

19. Wu Yaozong, 'Qingnian wenti tanzuo: xianshi yu chaoxianshi' [A topic for discussion amongst the youth: Reality and surreality], *Huanian* [Youthful years] Volume 4, Issue 6 (1935): 8–10.

XIANDAI [LES CONTEMPORAINS]: ALL SURREALISM UNDER HEAVEN

As previously mentioned, the editor of *Xiandai*, Shi Zhecun, refused a request from Eugène Jolas via Chinese expatriate Dai Wangshu, a poet and translator residing in France at the time, to dedicate a special edition of his journal to Surrealism. *Xiandai* has nevertheless left some important references to the Chinese Surrealist movement as well as contributing to its visual iconography in Shanghai. Jie helpfully frames *Xiandai* as a *tianxia* or 'all under heaven' publication which juxtaposed opposing viewpoints.[1] Indeed, in the first issue of *Xiandai* an article entitled *Cocktail de Shidai* [The era of the cocktail] by Xian Ming (1932), the author couches the alcoholic beverage as a metaphor for the 'new isms' emerging from the cityscape that have all been mixed together.[2] Surrealism is cited as part of this heady concoction, but the author ultimately rubbishes the movement, commenting that Breton's manifesto advocates 'destructive madness'.[3] Xian

1. Jie Shi, 'Xiandai zazhi and an Alternative Vision of Chinese Modernity' (PhD thesis, Newcastle University, 2017), 62.
2. Xian Ming, 'Cocktail de shidai' [The era of the cocktail], *Xiandai* 1 (1932): 166–74.
3. Xian, 'Cocktail de shidai'.

cites the events of the previously mentioned Saint-Pol-Roux banquet, concentrating on its violent elements (chairs were indeed thrown as the author notes).[4] Yet, the revolutionary, anti-colonial intent behind the Surrealists' brawl is omitted from Xian's account. The next mention of Surrealism, by the author Gao Ming, invokes its turn to communism in the fourth issue of the magazine and also notes the importance of the dissident Surrealist magazine *Documents* (1929–1930), edited by George Bataille, which he comments is focused heavily on folklore,[5] exhibiting an awareness of Surrealism's multi-faceted activity at this juncture.

While both derogatory and neutral text-based mentions of Surrealism existed in the first year of *Xiandai* magazine, between October 1933 and April 1934, the magazine's reception of the movement was distinctive due to a plethora of Surrealist front covers that populated the publication. Six consecutive front covers were created by the artists/cartoonists Pang Xunqin, Zhang Guangyu, Lei Guiyuan, Guo Jianying, Ye Lingfeng, and Zhou Duo.[6] First of all, Pang Xunqin created a front cover wherein two biomorphic bodies overlap, one reading a scroll ostensibly to demonstrate the literary nature of *Xiandai* magazine, the cursive line suggesting resonances with automatism as per Surrealist principles. Next, Zhang Guanyu's front cover presents two contorted grey bodies each wearing one shoe and the other wearing

4. Xian, 'Cocktail de shidai'.
5. Gao Ming, *Faguo wenyi zazhi* [French literature and art periodicals], *Xiandai* [Les Contemporains], 4 (1932): 35.
6. Hu Rong, 'Xiandai yishu tuanti Juelanshe yu "Xiandai" zazhi' [Modern art collective the Storm Society and Les Contemporains magazine], *Zhongguo xiandai wenxue yanjiu congkan* [Modern Chinese literature studies] 6 (2009): 95–103.

a seductive red dress, the malleability of form a common feature of Surrealism's corporeal representation. Both figures seem to be residing on some form of scroll or parchment in another allusion to the literary. Next, Lei Guiyuan enacts a Picasso-style rapid sketch of a naked woman riding two horses, the cyclops-like woman's curves are exaggerated with multiple lines rendering her somewhat three-dimensional, the Chinese cursive line again conducive to Surrealist automatism and the enactment of 'convulsive beauty'. Guo Jianying creates another automatic sketch of a woman portending more to commerciality by accentuating her accoutrements of gloves and lipstick. Ye Lingfeng's work is truly a synthesis of Surrealist symbols: seashells, fish, a distorted woman's face, and a glass of wine all appear on some torn sheets of paper in yet another form of meta-commentary which is also figured by a book in the centre of the composition. The symbol of the fish was originally used to advertise the Parisian 'Bureau of Surrealist Research' (1925) which acted as a public interface encouraging investigations into the subconscious through the recording of dream narratives from members of the public, perhaps portraying an absurdist deep-dive into the untapped realms of the psyche. Zhou Duo also uses the Surrealist fish and extrapolates it from its marine environment, positioning it against a brick wall and a garden in another absurd juxtaposition. Consequently, the *Xiandai* front covers very much portend to a revolution of the mind as opposed to society at large.

Given most of *Xiandai's* front covers were simply geometric patterns, the inclusion of Surrealist spreads at this juncture is highly intriguing. Much like *Xiandai*, which covered a wide range of opposing viewpoints, Surrealist artworks could also engender a variety of different reactions.

One thing these front covers were not, however, was political. Notwithstanding, the author Dai Wangshu,[7] who had studied abroad in Paris, attended the Association d'Écrivains et Artistes Révolutionnaires (Association of Revolutionary Writers and Artists) in March 1933, the atmosphere of which he regales in *Xiandai*. The gathering was filled with communist sympathisers protesting the rise of fascism in Germany, with many of its artists and writers such as the German artist much admired by Lu Xun, Käthe Kollwitz, thrown into prison. Dai notes the attendance of several Surrealists during the third day of proceedings (Louis Aragon, André Breton, René Char, René Crevel, Max Ernst, Pierre Unik, and Luis Buñuel).[8]

Only a few months later, in July 1933, the Surrealists were excluded from the Communist Party. The Surrealists' position is hard not to relate to what the author Du Heng (pseudonym Su Wen) had described as 'The Third Kind of Person'. Chinese Studies scholar and biographer of Dai Wangshu, Lee aptly resumes this figure as someone who '[w]hile accepting the Marxist view of history . . . denounces literary hegemony',[9] unable to accept party restrictions on creative practice. Su Wen had criticised the League of Left-Wing Writers, which was established in 1930 with the support of the Chinese Communist Party and counted Lu Xun among its ranks. In turn, Lu Xun, had written about his disdain for the 'Third Kind of Person' a year earlier in

7. Gregory Lee notes that Dai Wangshu met André Breton while in France; see Gregory B. Lee, *Dai Wangshu: The Life and Poetry of a Chinese Modernist* (Hong Kong: Chinese University of Hong Kong Press, 1989), 32.
8. Dai Wangshu, 'Faguo Tongxin' [Communiqué from France], *Xiandai* [Les Contemporains] 3, no. 2 (1933): 305–16.
9. Lee, *Dai Wangshu*, 37.

Xiandai (1932), while Dai Wangshu identified with such a figure.[10] Indeed, it is not hard to intuit parallels between the case of the Parisian Surrealists and those in Shanghai apropos 'fellow travellers' of Communism.

Although the concept of 'The Third Kind of Person' was forged in a literary framework, I would argue the same debate was being had in the Shanghainese artworld. Shi Zhecun defended the Storm Society (of which Pang Xunqin and Zhou Duo contributed front covers to *Xiandai*) against potent criticism from their peers after the Second Storm Society Exhibition of October 1933. This may well explain the reason for *Xiandai*'s string of Surrealist front covers at this juncture. Hu Rong notes the Storm Society exhibition had been criticised by a teacher at the Shanghai Art College.[11] In particular, Qiu Ti's non-realistic use of colour was singled out, as was Yang Taiyang's aforementioned Surrealist *Chimney and Mandolin* for its incongruous juxtapositions, counter to rational thinking. Shi noted that the teacher in question only praised a Storm Society painting by Liu Shi that portrayed a worker.[12] As such, it is clear that within left-wing circles, artists who leaned beyond representations of the proletariat were ripe for critique. In a literary sense, this is of course exactly what happened to Shi Zhecun, who aborted an introduction to Surrealism in 1934. This shows that beyond the oft-cited division between national painting and Western-style painting, another 'culture war' to use an anachronism, was afoot in Shanghai between avant-garde

10. Lee, *Dai Wangshu*, 32–33.
11. Hu, 'Xiandai yishu tuanti Juelanshe yu "Xiandai" zazhi' [Modern art collective the Storm Society and Les Contemporains magazine].
12. Hu, 'Xiandai yishu tuanti Juelanshe yu "Xiandai" zazhi'.

artists such as the Storm Society and revolutionary artists grouped around Lu Xun. Hu Rong states:

> The 'Surrealist Literature and Art Special Issue' immediately attracted harsh criticism from all parties, especially the left-wing camp that adhered to realism, this was more or less an inevitability. In order to ease any tension, Shi Zhecun chose to decline, and took the initiative to delay the official inauguration of 'Surrealism' in domestic literary and art media. It is not difficult to see the contradiction and compromise between Shi's personal interests and his public position.[13]

Consequently, *Xiandai* can be viewed as a publication that simultaneously promoted yet stymied Surrealism in Shanghai, its front covers visibly propagating a Surrealist style while delaying a fully-fledged special issue on the movement until the 1935 edition of *Yifeng*. While *Xiandai* and many other outlets made direct references to Surrealism, Surrealist photography, much like the Surrealist movement in Paris, was not elaborated with the same body of accompanying literature. However, it is undeniable that the visual impact of Surrealist photography held sway in Shanghai, encompassing both the satiation of individual desire and collective revolutionary endeavour as we will now turn to in the periodical *Modern Sketch*.

13, Hu, 'Xiandai yishu tuanti Juelanshe yu "Xiandai" zazhi'.

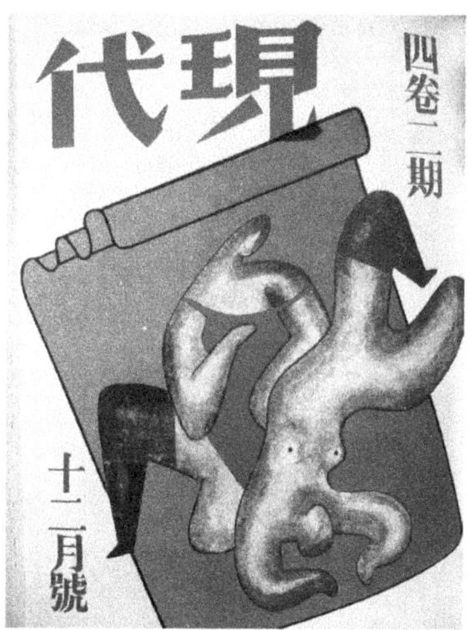

Figure 21. Zhang Guangyu (1933), Front cover for *Xiandai Magazine* [Les Contemporains] 4, no. 2 (1933). Photograph by the author.

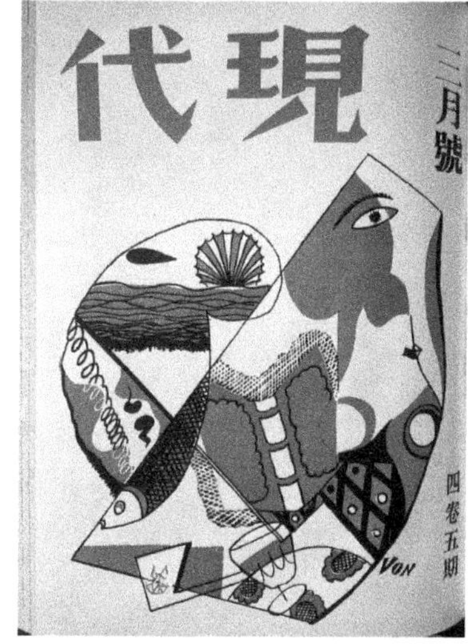

Figure 22. Ye Lingfeng (1934), Front cover for *Xiandai Magazine* [Les Contemporains] 4, no. 3 (1934). Photograph by the author.

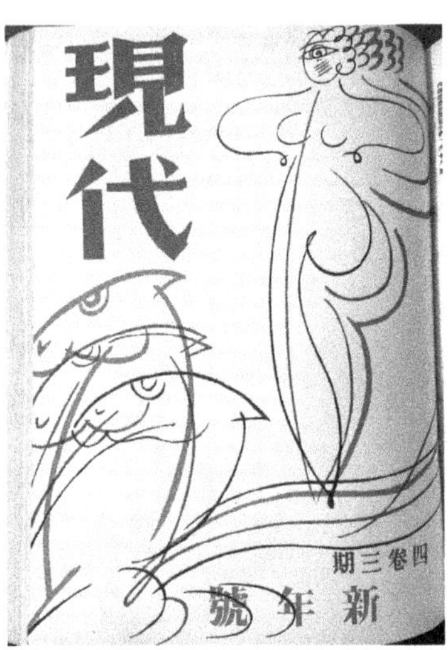

Figure 23. Lei Guiyuan (1934), Front cover for *Xiandai Magazine* [Les Contemporains] 4, no. 5 (1934). Photograph by the author.

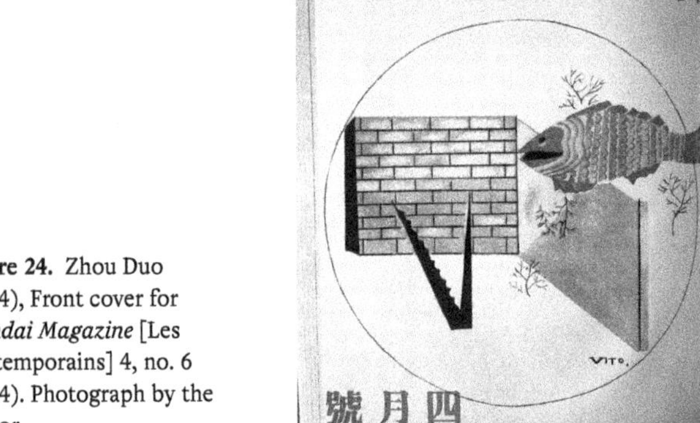

Figure 24. Zhou Duo (1934), Front cover for *Xiandai Magazine* [Les Contemporains] 4, no. 6 (1934). Photograph by the author.

SURREALIST PHOTOGRAPHY IN SHANGHAI: *SHIDAI MANHUA* [MODERN SKETCH]

Unlike the preponderantly aesthetic and Freudian leanings of avant-garde painting groups in Shanghai, usage of Surrealist photography was frequently political in nature. As Surrealist scholar Dawn Ades notes: 'Photomontage was increasingly used by all political factions in Europe and Russia in the decades before the Second World War . . . but it is not surprising that photomontage is particularly associated with the political Left, because it is ideally suited to the expression of the Marxist dialectic'.[1] The same can be said of the Chinese context. Indeed, the magazine *Shidai Manhua* [Modern sketch], a satirical journal that often employed photomontage to synthesise competing political or social phenomena at a time when Japan's colonial ambitions towards China reached their peak from 1934 to 1937. The journal was particularly Surrealist in its deployment of photographic

1. Dawn Ades, *Photomontage* (London: Thames and Hudson 1986), 41. This is not to say that the other aspects of Surrealism in Shanghai were not dialectic, in fact, I hope this volume proves they were simply dialectical in different ways.

appropriation. As Chinese cartoon expert Crespi notes: 'The Modern Publications office in fact has a photo studio on the third floor of its building on Shanghai's Hankou Lu,[2] to which the company would invite celebrities for photo shoots. The company also maintained its photo archive at this address, a resource that the editors of *Modern Sketch* could and did raid for material to be satirically repurposed.'[3] Photographic appropriation was a widely used technique in French Surrealist periodicals as Linda Steer has explored in her monograph on the subject. She notes: 'Surrealist photographic appropriation functions as an attack on the discursive frame that holds meaning in place.'[4] This is exactly the strategy that editors of *Shidai Manhua* utilised by expanding the discursive frame of a single photograph to a photomontage in order to convey the paradox of a city simultaneously embroiled in hedonistic vice concurrent to the very real threat of Japanese aggression.

In the first issue of *Shidai Manhua* in 1934 an anonymous piece entitled *Shanghai Fengjing* [Shanghai landscape] comprises a particularly terse parody of unbridled excess. Paul Bevan has convincingly argued that this work was directly inspired by George Grosz's *American Landscape* (1933).[5] Admittedly, Grosz was much more closely connected to Dadaism than Surrealism and this is not something I wish to challenge. Yet, from a historiographic perspective, Dadaism

2. Formerly known as Customs House Road.
3. John A. Crespi, 'China's Modern Sketch: The Golden Era of Cartoon Art, 1934–1937', *MIT Visualising Cultures*, accessed 2 May 2024, https://visualizingcultures.mit.edu/modern_sketch/ms_essay_03.pdf.
4. Linda Steer, *Appropriated Photographs in French Surrealist Periodicals, 1924–1939* (Abingdon: Routledge 2017), 154.
5. Paul Bevan, *A Modern Miscellany: Shanghai Cartoon Artists, Shao Xunmei's Circle, and the Travels of Jack Chen 1926–1938* (Leiden: Brill, 2016), 158–59.

had all but merged into the Surrealist movement by 1933 which began to gain popularity in the United States during the 1930s (Grosz moved there in 1933 after Hitler's accession to power in Germany). Secondly, Dadaism was frequently criticised for its nihilistic tendencies and lack of political engagement, something the fervent satire and left-wing ideological critique of Grosz's photomontage does not abide by. As such, the politico-subjectivism of Grosz, himself a former communist party member who in 1933 repudiated communism, as well as his use of photomontage, could be said to be very much akin to the trajectory and artistic practice of many Surrealists, so much so that Grosz's work was admired and indeed, collected by André Breton. His piece *The Funeral* (1917–1918) featured as part of an International Surrealist Exhibition 'L'Ecart Absolu' in 1965.[6]

Schaefer comments that the piece, *Shanghai Fengjing*, is 'composed of the signifiers of a colonial modernity, ranging from gambling (money, cards, mah-jongg tiles) and stimulants (alcohol and opium) to fashionable shoes, guns, and a Sikh policeman'.[7] These elements depict Shanghai as a hedonistic city, also dubbed a 'paradise of adventurers' where every desire could be satiated upon payment. The impeding threat from Japan lingers in the background through weaponry. The Sikh policeman was a prominent figure in the International Settlement, recruited from India in a British colonial context. This figure further connotes the contradictions between cosmopolitanism and colonialism in the Shanghai cityscape while disjointed and fetishised body

6. *L'Écart absolu* [The gaping void] 1965 Catalogue de l'Exposition: Galerie de L'Œil.
7. William Schaefer, *Shadow Modernism: Photography, Writing, and Space in Shanghai, 1925–1937* (Durham, NC: Duke University Press, 2017), 155.

parts further augment the Surrealist nature of this piece from a psychoanalytic angle. Situating this work in the context of the periodical as a whole, this hedonistic image was juxtaposed with disturbing political content alerting viewers to the rise of fascism via the figures of Mussolini and Hitler, containing an image of a Nazi salute entitled 'Another new front?' [*xinzhenxian*] commingling the popularisation of a genocidal regime with new clothing styles and recreational pastimes. Indeed, another collage-style piece was entitled 'insomnia' [*shiyanzheng*], parodying the array of night-club shows available in Shanghai. The first issue of *Shidai Manhua* undoubtedly demonstrated that any semblance of everyday reality within this cityscape was a highly unstable commodity.

By 1936, *Shidai Manhua* was even more strident in depicting political instability. Another anonymous photomontage *Biaozhun Zhongguoren* [A standard Chinese man], utilises the same Surrealist principle of photographic appropriation by expanding the discursive frame of a regular photograph to include disparate elements that nevertheless made up the cacophony of everyday reality in 1930s China. Here, Chinese and imperialist iconography clash. The *Standard Chinese Man* is carrying a traditional wicker basket on his back, signifying his burden of responsibility, the

Figure 25. Anon., *Shanghai Landscape* (1934), photomontage, in *Shidai Manhua* [Modern sketch] 1 (1934): 23. Courtesy of the Special Collections and University Archives, Colgate University Libraries.

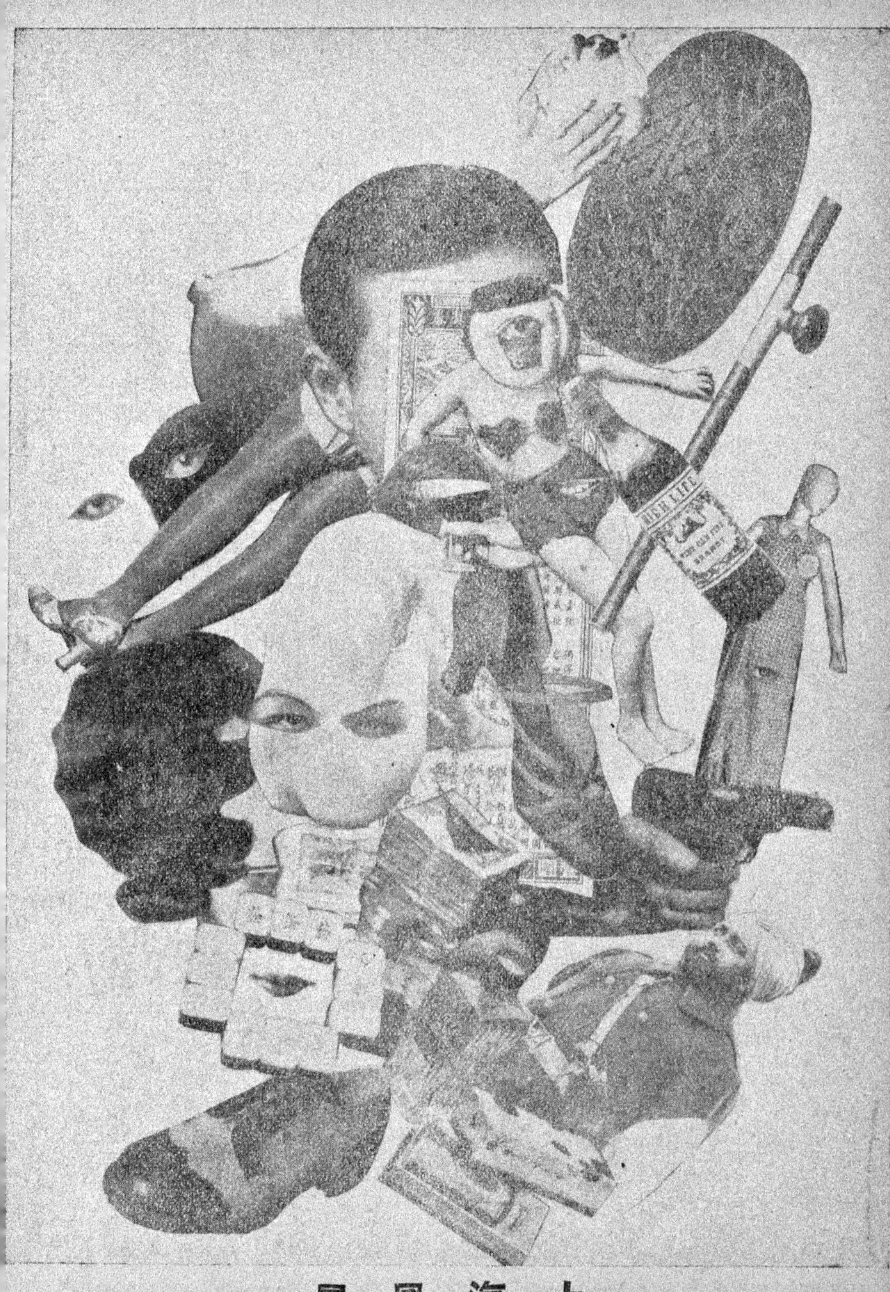

上海風景

basket containing two innocent crying children. A pagoda embodies indigenous culture, while we are confronted with a Confucian sage in a meditative pose and a cooking pot, upon which Japanese planes drop bombs from above. Tape is pasted over the man's mouth, gesturing towards inertia and an inability to speak. From below, an electricity pylon is keeling over, connoting damage to China's fledgling infrastructure, while an arsenal of military artillery is poised to attack from the lower right of the composition. Curiously, the man is cupping a Western female nude, ostensibly an attempt to cling on to the heady atmosphere of the *années folles* that are under threat. The man's trousers are covered in newspaper print; most of the Chinese characters are too small to read, however, one headline appears to concern airline shares while the other has clearly visible characters that read *liu xue* or 'blood flows', perhaps in an attempt to depict how everyday life is somehow continuing despite the imminent threat of fully fledged war and massacre.

Possibly the most disturbing photomontage in *Modern Sketch* bears the hallmarks of Dalí-esque influence. The bare trees that haunt the image seem reminiscent of Salvador Dalí's *The Persistence of Memory* (1931). *Hung by the Heels of Hell* was created by Wang Zimei in the very last issue of *Shidai Manhua* in June 1937 before the outbreak of the Second Sino-Japanese War the following month. Wang uses the Surrealist technique of incongruous juxtaposition to offset a 'modern girl' female star turned upside down as if she is diving into a sea of hanging cadavers. The verticality of both the corpses and the modern girl aesthetically mirrors two distinct realities of life in Shanghai that collided on a daily basis: colonial modernity and the imminent threat of war.

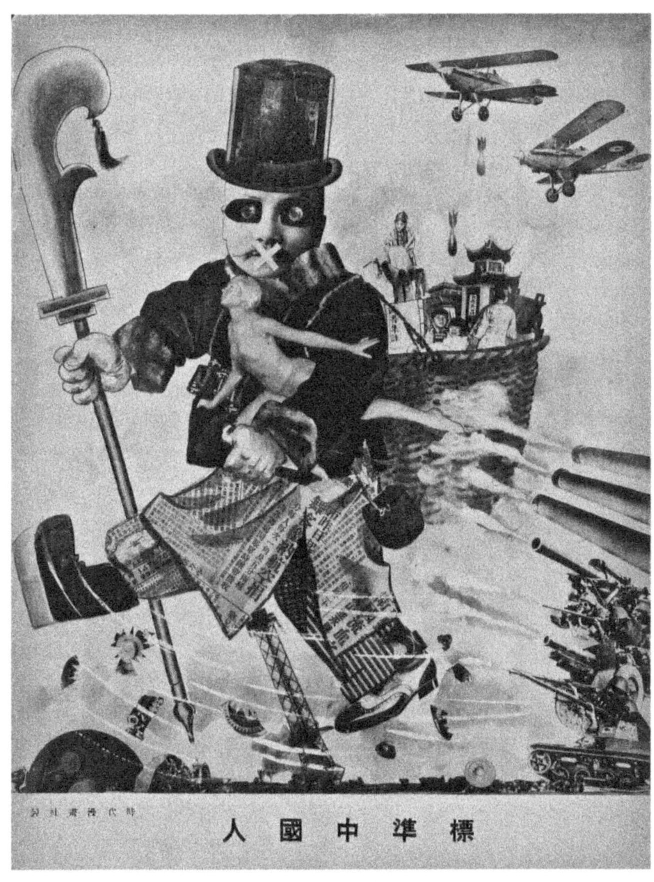

Figure 26. Anon., *A Standard Chinese Man* (1936), photomontage, in *Shidai Manhua* [Modern sketch] 25 (1936): 20. Courtesy of the Special Collections and University Archives, Colgate University Libraries.

In December 1936, the leader of the Nationalist Party, Chiang Kai-shek, was kidnapped and forced to enter into a united front with the Communists against the Japanese in what became known as the Xi'an Incident. Chiang had formally persecuted the Communists over and above countering Japanese aggression under his policy *an nei rang wai* [pacify the internal threat before the external]. This meant that the outbreak of war was inevitable – it was only a question of when. As such, this final issue of *Shidai Manhua*, while containing some jovial moments, is much bleaker in its outlook, including a spread juxtaposing pretty porcelain dolls and starving children. Less than a month after the issue was published, war broke out on 7 July 1937. Shanghai's *années folles*, with its seemingly ubiquitous array of 'modern girls', came to an abrupt end.

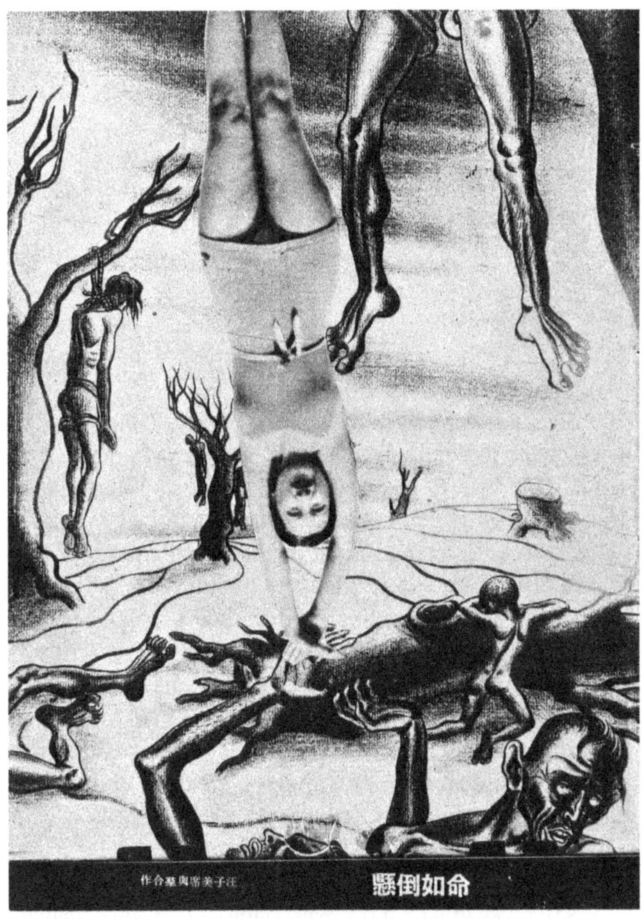

Figure 27. Wang Zimei (1937), *Hung by the Heels of Hell*, photomontage, in *Shidai Manhua* [Modern sketch] 39 (1937): 10. Courtesy of the Special Collections and University Archives, Colgate University Libraries.

SURREALIST PHOTOGRAPHY IN SHANGHAI: LANG JINGSHAN (1892–1995)

Like the photomontages of *Modern Sketch*, Lang Jingshan also blended photography with other art forms, aligning with Surrealism's history of photographic invention. Shanghai is where Lang Jingshan's photographic practice began in the 1920s, his career being forged in the newspapers and periodicals of the city before transitioning into artistic photography. Unlike the Storm Society and their torchbearer Pang Xunqin, it appears that Lang Jingshan principally borrowed from the photographic techniques of Surrealism rather than its ideological convictions. In stark contrast to the hybrid art of Pang Xunqin for example, there was a greater sense of 'Chineseness' in Lang's photographic oeuvre. In turn, this made his photography more marketable to the West, conserving a level of exoticism in terms of its reception there. As Gruzinski notes: 'Exoticism is simply a purveyor of clichés . . . it's the way in which the West habitually stamps its mark all over the world.'[1] Yet, to counter this inevitable surge of exoticism in the cosmopolitan yet colonial environment of

1. Serge Gruzinski, *La Pensée métissée* (Paris: Fayard, 2012), 22.

Shanghai, Lang Jingshan, with two other friends, even set up a small society named *Sanyou Yinghui*, which roughly translates as 'Photography Society of Three Friends'. The society bore the explicit aim of exhibiting their Chinese photography in international salons in order to dispel outmoded myths about Chinese culture, indeed Lang Jingshan stated the *Sanyou Yinghui* strove: 'to correct the erroneous concepts foreigners have towards Chinese society'.[2] Hence, Lang utilises photography as a form of Chinese cultural diplomacy to dismiss prevailing notions of exoticism during the modernist era.

A 1939 exhibition catalogue of Lang Jingshan's photography at L'Université de L'Aurore in the French Concession proudly emphasises the number of works he managed to show abroad, an accolade not attained by the Storm Society.[3] In the catalogue, Wong stated: 'Within nine years, he has exhibited 755 pictures.'[4] It transpires that in Paris alone between 1932 and 1938 Lang Jingshan had eleven prints exhibited. Lang Jingshan himself never studied abroad for an extended period, however he did travel abroad for exhibitions and his studio was located in Shanghai's French Concession, the

2. Gang Cheng, *Lang Jingshan Zhuan* (Nanjing: Jiangsu renmin chubanshe, 2012), 103.
3. Although the Second Sino-Japanese War had broken out by this point, foreign concessions were not initially targeted by the Japanese. However, the International Settlement was occupied in December 1941 after Japan's entrance into the Second World War following the attack on Pearl Harbor. Shanghai's French Concession was not subject to occupation by the Japanese throughout the Second World War due to the Vichy government's allegiance with axis powers.
4. Lewis L. Wong, 'Appendix' in Chin-San Long, Association Photographique de l'Université l'Aurore, Shanghai (China). Université l'Aurore, *Exhibition of Pictorial Photography: To Commemorate the Centenary of Daguèrre* (Shanghai: [publisher not identified], 1939), 24.

hub of modernist cultural activity in Shanghai. Indeed, *The North China Herald* reported that 'Mr Chin San-Long[5] holds a foremost place amongst Chinese photographic artists, and his studio in Frenchtown is filled with exquisite studies, many of which have gained awards at exhibits in Europe.'[6] As such, Lang Jingshan led a thoroughly cosmopolitan existence in the sense of Partha Mitter's aforementioned 'virtual cosmopolis', which was 'achieved by means of global print culture. Colonial hegemonic languages, English, French, and Spanish, circulated through print culture, created conditions for communication between center and periphery, giving rise to an imagined community, namely, a "virtual cosmopolis"'.[7] Indeed, the presence of surrealist happenings in the French Concession, mainly disseminated through periodicals, and partially through exhibitions, doubtless infiltrated his work.

As Ge Siming and Lin Mingmei note, Lang Jingshan's daughter, Eve Long, took over the management of her father's photographs and negatives comprising almost one hundred years of previously unpublished material.[8] Lang Jingshan and surrealist photographer Man Ray met in Paris in 1960 during a photography conference and once again in 1974. Lang also accessed Man Ray's 70 different exhibitions in France's national library. Lang's archives hold a photograph of Man Ray and his business card.[9] However,

5. This is another common way to Romanise 'Lang Jingshan' or 郎静山.
6. *North China Herald* (1850–1940) (Leiden: Brill, 1935), 292.
7. Keith Moxey and Partha Mitter, 'A "Virtual Cosmopolis": Partha Mitter in Conversation with Keith Moxey', *The Art Bulletin* 95, no. 3 (2013): 381–92.
8. Ge Siming and Lin Mingmei, *Mingjia mingliu mingshi Lang Jingshan shishinian zhounian jinian wenji* [Famous faces: An essay collection to commemorate the 20th anniversary of Lang Jingshan's passing] (Taibei: Guoli lishi bowuguan, 2015), 264.
9. Ge and Lin, *Mingjia mingliu mingshi Lang Jingshan*, 264.

Man Ray's influence on Lang Jingshan most likely began in the early 1930s, which is apparent through iconographical comparisons of their respective works, coupled with awareness of Man Ray and Surrealism in Republican Shanghai at the time via numerous periodicals. For example, Man Ray's *Le Violon d'Ingres* (1924) was published in the popular magazine *Shidai Huabao* [Modern miscellany].

In 1974, Man Ray wrote to Lang Jingshan from Paris: 'I paint what cannot be photographed. I photograph what cannot be painted.'[10] Indeed, Danzker stresses: 'experimentation by Chinese artists in the 1920s and 1930s, in China and abroad, within both foreign and indigenous traditions, can also be described as a resolute search for new techniques'.[11] Importantly, one of the surrealist features attributed to Lang Jingshan is his photographic experimentation. In 1934, he created 'composite photography' [*Jijin Sheying*],[12] which Chinese art historian Lu Huan describes thus: 'there is painting in photography and photography in painting'.[13] Although Lang Jingshan amalgamates photography and painting into a single frame, parallels can readily be drawn with the innovations of surrealist photomontage along with Man Ray's rayograms, solarisations, decalcomania and so on. Ge and Lin state: 'It could even be said that the thematic relation of Lang Jingshan's oeuvre to Surrealism happens to be the same, especially important is the possession of

10. Ge and Lin, *Mingjia mingliu mingshi Lang Jingshan*, 264.
11. Jo-Anne Birnie Danzker, Ken Lum, and Zheng Shengtian, *Shanghai Modern: 1919–1945* (Ostfildern-Ruit: Hatje Cantz, 2004), 64.
12. Lang explained the methodology behind composite photography in the *Journal of the Royal Photographic Society* in February 1942 entitled 'Composite Pictures and Chinese Art'.
13. Lu Huan, 'Lang Jingshan de Sheying Meixue Sixiang', *Journal of Mianyang Normal University* 29, no. 9 (2010): 27.

unrelenting new creation and experimental innovation.'[14] As such, Lang's efforts resemble those of Euro-American artists who turned to non-Western cultures as a source of inspiration, new formal languages, and above all new techniques which they then adapted for their needs in order to reform and revitalise their own cultural traditions. This is not to say that Lang's composite photography and surrealist photomontage are one and the same. On the contrary, Lang's work emphasises more of a seamless transition between photography and painting, instigating a harmony of different techniques and pictorial forms, whereas surrealist photomontage gives rise to disjuncture and the incongruous juxtapositions that characterise the movement's resolution of opposing forces.

Notwithstanding, the most evident point of comparison between Lang Jingshan and Man Ray is undoubtedly in their treatment of the female nude and the juxtaposing of nude models with sacred objects. In 1928, Lang was the first Chinese to photograph a nude female which incited substantial controversy at the time. In her pioneering work on nudes in Shanghainese pictorials, Waara, an expert on gender history, states that Chinese culture, similarly to the West, was dominated by the male gaze, while nudes are frequently represented in a passive manner – the female is publicly exhibited whilst the voyeur is granted anonymity.[15]

Lang's first nude photograph was entitled *Appreciate* [*Shendu wusi*], the title in English mitigating somewhat any

14. Ge and Lin, *Mingjia mingliu mingshi: Lang Jingshan shishinian zhounian jinian wenji* (Taibei: Guoli lishi bowuguan, 2015), 153.
15. Carrie Waara, 'The Bare Truth: Nudes, Sex, and the Modernization Project in Shanghai Pictorials', in *Visual Culture in Shanghai*: 1850s–1930s, ed. Jason C. Kuo (Washington, DC: New Academia Publishing, 2007), 192.

sense of libidinous purposes and connoting its status as a work of fine art. Nonetheless, this daring gesture faced a substantial backlash from the more conservative elements in Shanghai. According to a newspaper article, the model depicted in the photograph 'suffered brutal kicks and blows from her father who heard it four days later, as nude modelling at that time was regarded as shameful'.[16] Hence, it is clear that the nude as form infiltrated Shanghai from modern Western art, rather than having ancient origins in Chinese culture.

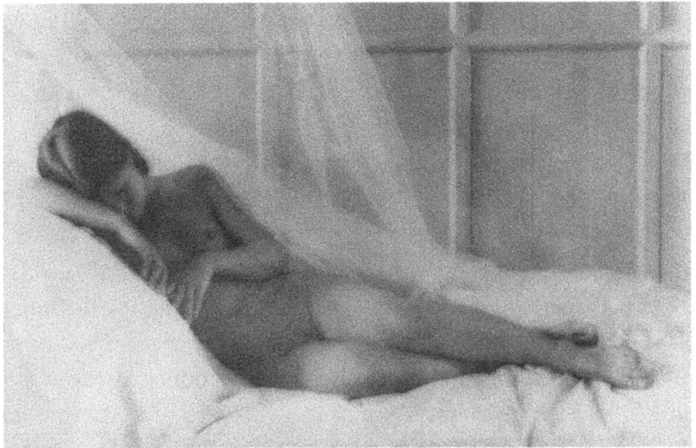

Figure 28. Lang Jingshan (1928), *Appreciate*, photograph, 25.6 × 39.4 cm, in *A Selection of Idyllic Composite Pictures by Prof. Chin San-Long* (Taipei: Photographic Society of China, 1990), unpaginated. Courtesy of the Long Chin-San Foundation.

16. Zhang Junmian, 'China's First Nude Photographer' (2013), accessed 30 March 2018, https://www.globaltimes.cn/content/828667.shtml.

Despite this backlash, Lang continued to shoot nude models and such works were published in a wide range of Shanghainese periodicals. In *Nirvanesque* (1930s), a nude woman is holding a statue of a Buddha's head with her legs crossed in a lotus meditative position, immersed introspectively in her own thoughts. The statue is cupped by her breasts and the lighting creates a cloud-like, floating background, symbolising that the state of Nirvana, a state of untrammelled happiness, has been reached. In this case, a sense of reciprocal happiness is attained by both the photographed entity and the viewer, the woman introspectively glances downwards. Perhaps Waara's commentary on Lang Jingshan could be slightly nuanced; while a hegemonic male gaze certainly persists outside the camera lens, the woman is presented as having found emancipation from the drudgeries of daily life.

Conversely, Man Ray's nude photographs are much more overt catalysts for the viewer's pleasure. In the 1927 photograph, *Simone Kahn with Vanuatu Male Figure*, Kahn[17] directly confronts the camera lens while the artefact looms over her with a clearly crafted phallus whose positioning could be viewed as a cipher for intercourse. The painting in the background betrays an art gallery context, therefore allusions to performativity and the complicity of the model could ensue. Here, the spirituality of the artefact Kahn

17. Simone Kahn married founder of Surrealism André Breton in 1921. They separated a decade later after Simone had an affair with the artist Max Morise. Kahn had been vital in supporting Breton's efforts as an art dealer. For more information, consult Vérane Tasseau, 'Simone Breton (née Kahn, also Simone Collinet)', The Modern Art Index Project (September 2018), Leonard A. Lauder Research Center for Modern Art, The Metropolitan Museum of Art, accessed 2 May 2024, https://www.metmuseum.org/research-centers/leonard-a-lauder-research-center/research-resources/modern-art-index-project/breton-simone.

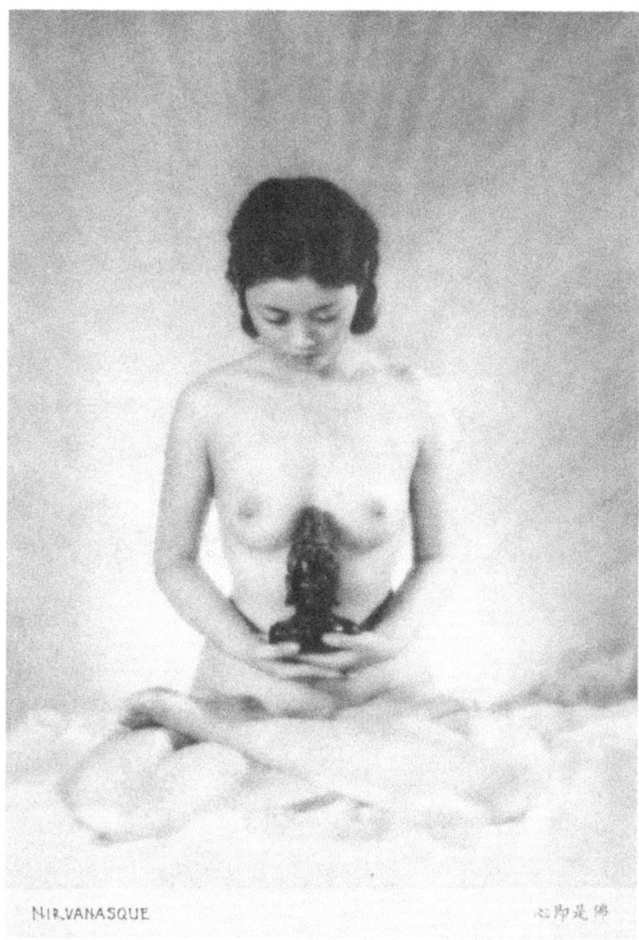

Figure 29. Lang Jingshan (1930s), *Nirvanesque*, photograph, dimensions unknown, in *Exhibition of Pictorial Photography by Chin-San Long: To Commemorate the Centenary of Daguèrre* (1939), Plate 86. Courtesy of the Long Chin-San Foundation.

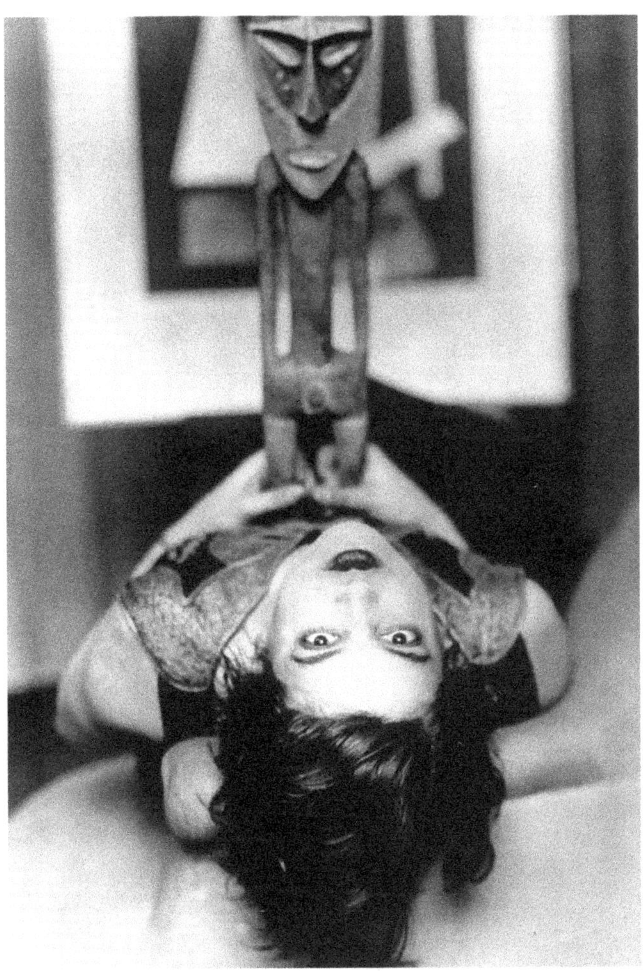

Figure 30. Man Ray (1927), *Simone Kahn with Vanuatu Male Figure*, photograph 29.4 × 10.7 cm. Centre Pompidou Paris. © Man Ray 2015 Trust / DACS, London 2024.

is photographed with is essentialised. Conversely, Lang Jingshan's chosen background is the celestial realm, the state of Nirvana in Buddhist terms resembling a heaven on earth. Lai notes that Lang Jingshan was indeed a Buddhist from childhood. Sexuality is therefore somewhat attenuated by the sense of the model's meditative modality.

A striking difference between Lang's photography and that of Man Ray is a deliberate occultation of the gaze. The models not only turn away but seem to disdain the very presence of the camera lens as an unwanted intrusion into their private realm of existence. A prime example of this is a 1932 photograph entitled *Through the Leaf Pattern*. In order to make this image, Lai notes that for this photograph, Lang 'printed two negatives on the same sheet of photographic paper'.[18] Indeed, Lang superimposes a diaphanous leaf membrane with its natural patterning of veins and ridges framing the nude body of Lang's model. The leaf seems to reference Christian biblical imagery of modesty after the fall of Adam and Eve and the onset of shame. In terms of religious connotations, Lai cites an essay by Lang Jingshan regarding nude photography where he states: 'When we talk about nude photography, we will firstly think of Adam and Eve. They are the most beautiful and perfect human figures created by God, and also the inexhaustible source of inspiration for the painters'.

After the invention of photography, it has also become a popular topic for the art photographers. This is because the human body is made of beautiful and soft lines, which under different lighting conditions will express the purest level

18. Edwin Kin-keung Lai, 'The Life and Art Photography of Lang Jingshan (1892–1995)' (PhD thesis, University of Hong Kong, 2000), 203.

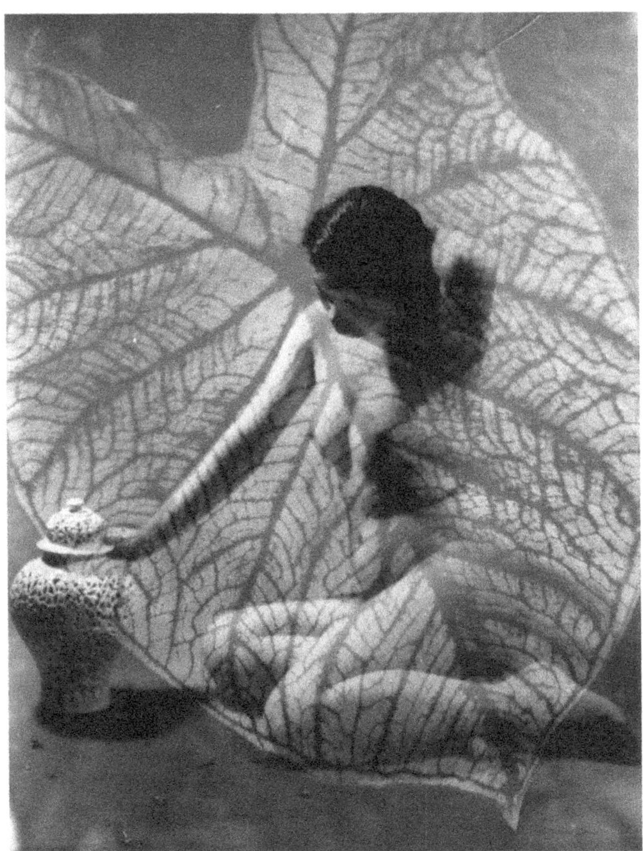

Figure 31. Lang Jingshan (1932), *Through the Leaf Pattern*, black and white 25.2 × 20.1 cm. Courtesy of the Long Chin-San Foundation.

of truth, beauty and virtue.[19] As such, it is clear that Lang Jingshan is equating nudity with spirituality and rational visions of beauty or as surrealist scholar and artist Fijalkoski aptly puts it: 'Classical concepts of beauty are based above all on an appreciation of ideal human form and privilege symmetry, order and proportion.'[20] This is somewhat polarised from André Breton's infamous surrealist notion of 'convulsive beauty' based on violence and spontaneity.[21] Indeed, the location of Simone Kahn in an art gallery in a sexually provocative pose, subjugated to an object, certainly fits with this characterisation.

By rendering the leaf transparent, Lang transgresses the private realm and the sense of shame through revealing the sequestered universe of the female subject. She appears to be styling her hair with one hand resting on an urn, a highly subversive, quasi-necrophiliac gesture. The urn in Buddhist culture though was synonymous with funereal rituals and would contain the ashes of a loved one. One could argue Lang uses syncretic religious imagery to create a memento mori and an ecumenical passage from life to death, from the early realisation of shame to our inevitable demise. Nevertheless, the commingling of different religious symbols also entails a cosmopolitan transcendence of national boundaries, very much in keeping with the atmosphere of modernist Shanghai.

It appears that the initial outcry at Lang Jingshan's 1928 photograph *Appreciate* is something that he would later parody in his corpus of nudes during the 1930s. In 1935, Lang published a nude in the pictorial magazine *Meishu*

19. Lai, 'The Life and Art Photography of Lang Jingshan', 200.
20. Krzysztof Fijalkowski and Michael Richardson, eds., *Surrealism: Key Concepts* (New York: Routledge, 2016), 184.
21. Fijalkowski and Richardson, *Surrealism*, 186.

Shenghuo [Arts and life] The Chinese title of this photograph is simply *renti* or *Human Figure*. However, it is translated into English as *Shameful*. As such, it appears that Lang Jingshan is creating a ludic contrast of differing cultural preconceptions. The model is completely concealing her face, rendering herself wholly anonymous. She is shrouded in a dark shade; the contours of her body are interrupted in a gesture of self-protection, her other hand wrapped around her waist. Such a pose would be anathema to the Western ideal of nudity as emancipation and beauty. Hence, Lang is informing the Western viewer of the Shanghainese social context while encouraging the Shanghainese viewer to merely consider the photograph a normative rendering of the human body. Lang published another photograph in *Arts and Life*, also in 1935, entitled *Huidao Ziran* [Back to nature] a faithful and literal translation in this instance. The photograph depicts two nude women sojourning beside a tree, in a bucolic setting. Dishevelled hair adds to the naturalistic pose Lang wishes to capture, ostensibly eschewing Man Ray's predilection for performativity.

Specifically, regarding the nude, Man Ray states: 'The nude is always in fashion,'[22] granting the subject a sense of atemporality. He doesn't abide by any strict rules or regulations. In stark contrast, Waara cites Lang Jingshan's attitude towards nudes in his 'Talk on the History of Photography': 'According to Lang, the "rules" for photographing nudes differed among some countries, but the focus was not supposed to be on a woman's crotch, nor should the subject's

22. Jennifer Mundy, ed., *Man Ray: Writings on Art* (London: Tate Publishing, 2016), 365.

attitude be libidinous.'[23] While Man Ray views the nude as a universal, atemporal phenomenon, for Lang the nude is bound by social context and tradition. Indeed, since Lang's models do not face the camera, the libidinous aspect of these photographs is attenuated somewhat, although a sense of transgression is undeniably present.

Lang took a boat to Taiwan in 1949 during the communist takeover of mainland China with the leader of the nationalist government Chiang Kai-shek. In so doing, he firmly nailed his political colours to the mast. His appropriation of Man Ray's surrealist techniques, however, deepened even further in Taiwan in comparison to his time in Shanghai's French Concession, as demonstrated by his use of rayography to convey what appears to be a composite reworking of his 1932 piece *Through the Leaf Pattern*. The outline of the nude clutching an urn is positioned atop the photographic negative with the sinuosity of the leaf contouring the model's body, integrating it with nature's own hypnotic patterning. The piece is ironically entitled *Long Matured in the Bottle*, making an analogy to wine. It seems that Lang is joking that the technical innovation of rayography took a long time for him to assimilate into his photographic repertoire. Indeed, I have not myself come across a reproduction of a rayography in 1930s Shanghai periodicals.

Beyond Man Ray, Ge and Lin note Lang also conserved, a photograph of Marcel Duchamp in his personal archives, who was arguably one of the surrealists most readily in dialogue with Freudian psychoanalysis.[24] A particularly Freudian artistic convergence can be made between Lang

23. Waara, 'The Bare Truth', 192.
24. Ge and Lin, *Mingjia mingliu mingshi Lang Jingshan*, 264.

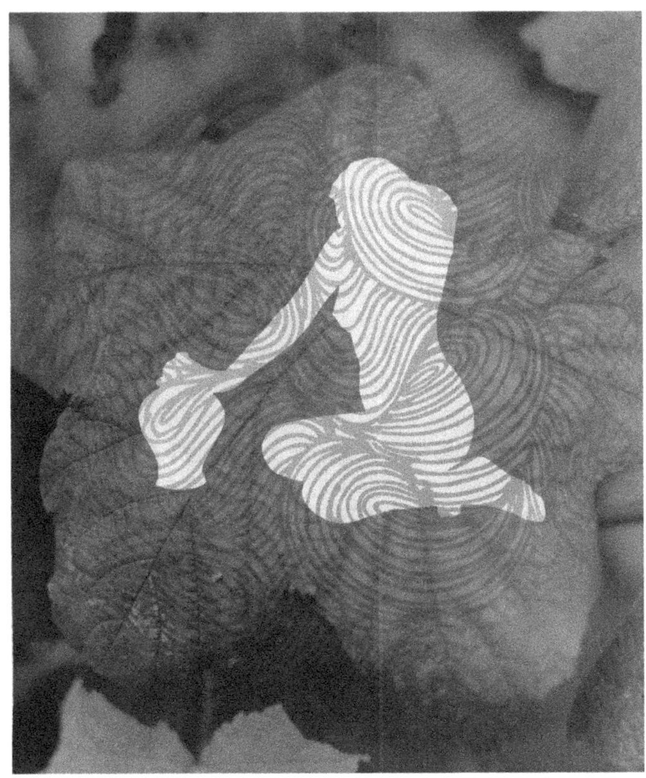

Figure 32. Lang Jingshan (1960s), *Long Matured in the Bottle* (rayography) 61 × 50.3 cm. Taipei, Private Collection. Courtesy of the Long Chin-San Foundation.

Jingshan's androgynous photo for *Shidai Huabao* [Modern miscellany] a Shanghai-based periodical and a work of one of his inspirational sources, Marcel Duchamp's alter-ego Rrose Sélavy, photographed by Man Ray. The title in Chinese *Yaotiao Shunan* (1933) can be translated literally as 'graceful man'. *Modern Miscellany* was one of the many journals Lang Jingshan photographed for during his early career in Shanghai. The journal clearly promotes androgyny as a cultural phenomenon, the model is nonchalant, autonomous, and self-assured. The botanical background offers an idiosyncratically Chinese setting amid otherwise Western attire, while the braces seem to suggest a professional career and the cigarette a high salary, with more and more women gaining professional roles. Indeed, regarding the figure of the so-called 'Modern Girl' in Shanghai, International Studies scholar Dong states:

> The emergence of an urban culture targeting the young opened up space for single young women to play new roles in society. These public roles for women involved unprecedented visibility and shifts in representation, including Modern Girl fashions, attitudes, and images.[25]

Indeed, within avant-garde circles, androgyny and cross-dressing were accepted facets of performing gender in Shanghai during the 1930s. Notwithstanding, Luo notes 'Female cross-dressing is hardly a Western importation into modern China. There has been a long history of female

25. Madelaine Dong, 'Who's Afraid of the Chinese Modern Girl?', in *The Modern Girl around the World: Consumption, Modernity, and Globalization*, ed. The Modern Girl around the World Research Group, Alys Eve Weinbaum, Lynn M. Thomas, Priti Ramamurthy, Uta G. Poiger, Madeleine Yue Dong, and Tani E. Barlow (Durham, NC: Duke University Press, 2008), 195.

cross-dressing in premodern Chinese literary tradition dating back to Mulan.'[26] Indeed, Luo also alludes to the contemporaneous figure of Tian Han who 'was a multi-faceted male figure . . . a playful cross-dressing modern girl in Tokyo in the early 1920s, to the emergence of a powerful femme fatale on the silver screen in Shanghai in the late 1920s'.[27] For Duchamp, androgyny and cross-dressing were a performative trope, to manifest everything that could be considered 'other', conveying the mutable nature of one's own identity.

In short, Lang Jingshan utilised surrealist tropes and techniques but firmly clung on to a sense of Chinese national identity in his work, utilising conventional tropes of nature, and spiritual and rational beauty, rather than the surrealist envisioning of beauty as convulsive. Lang Jingshan was fervently aware of the limitations of his social context and so, in order to break boundaries, Lang mitigated the effects of his most daring gestures, he photographed the first Chinese nude but in a meditative rather than performative pose. He surrounded his nudes in natural settings replete with Chinese symbolism and even had recourse to religious iconography in order to attenuate his daring gesture with notions of purity. While Man Ray's juxtapositions are deliberately incongruous, Lang's associations of nudity with Chinese art-historical staples such as Buddhist elements would be unsurprising in a Chinese context, although such iconography could form more exotic connotations to Western eyes. Lang's androgynous woman is endowed with far greater autonomy than his nudes, most of whom seem to be in a state of meditative

26. Liang Luo, 'Modern Girl, Modern Men, and the Politics of Androgyny in Modern China', *Michigan Quarterly Review* 47, no. 2: *China* (Spring 2008), accessed 2 May 2024, http://hdl.handle.net/2027/spo.act2080.0047.223.

27. Luo, 'Modern Girl, Modern Men'.

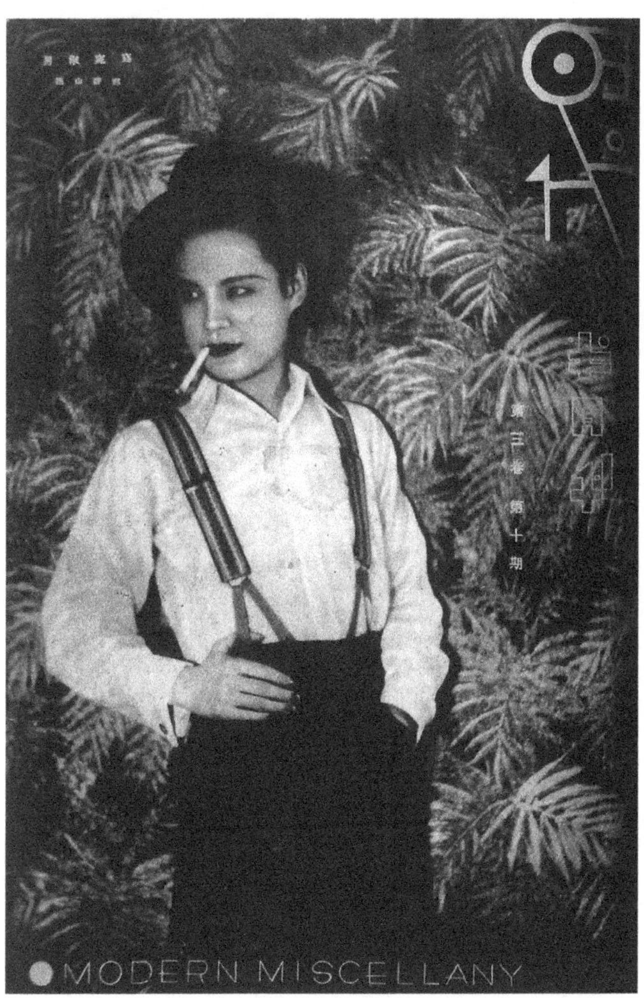

Figure 33. Lang Jingshan (1933), Front cover, *Yaotiao Shunan* in *Shidai Huabao* [Modern miscellany]. Courtesy of the Long Chin-San Foundation.

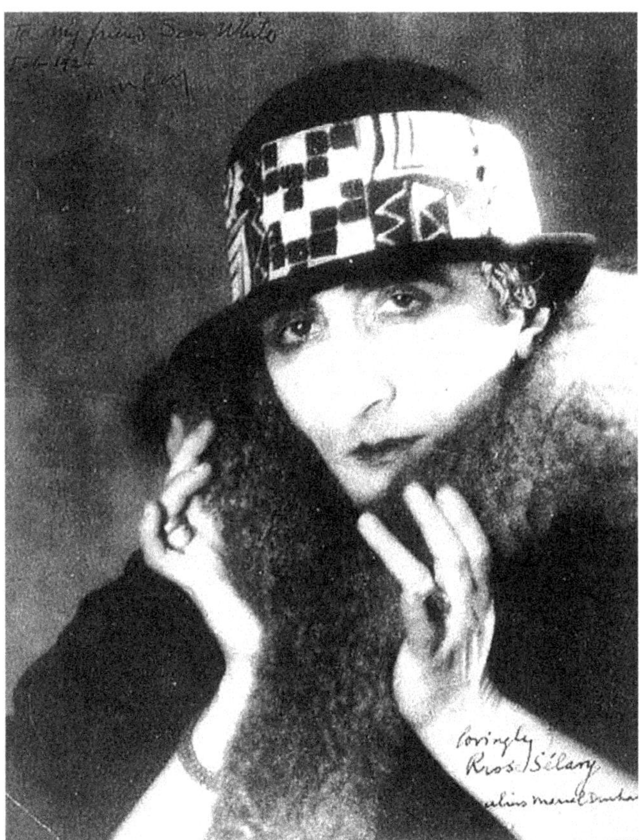

Figure 34. Marcel Duchamp and Man Ray (1921), *Rrose Selavy*, photograph retouched by Marcel Duchamp, 13.8 × 9.9 cm. Smithsonian Donald W. Reynolds Centre, Washington. © Succession Marcel Duchamp/ADAGP, Paris and DACS, London / © Man Ray Trust/ADAGP, Paris and DACS, London 2024.

contemplation, his 'new woman' rather shows his engagement with the woman as subject rather than object. There is a sense of empirical socio-political change that is being conveyed on *Modern Miscellany* magazine's front cover, but this tendency, although other examples exist, is less overt in Lang's corpus as a whole. Hence, it is clear then that Lang was not an ardent fellow traveller of Surrealism in terms of its politics and philosophy, moreso its artistry. What is certain though, is that Lang Jingshan's Surrealism superseded his time in Shanghai's French Concession, and he continued his practice in Taiwan under the Nationalist party and martial law, Surrealism combining with an idiosyncratically Chinese expression of desire that could circumnavigate censorship in spite of its culturally controversial subject matter.

CONCLUSION

The pervasive presence of Surrealism in Shanghai during the mid-1930s can be attributed to a wide-range of social, cultural, and political factors; a yearning for national renewal, the stagnancy of the *guohua* genre, anti-colonial protest, the rise of Western individualism, desire, circumnavigating censorship, and perhaps most universally, the steadfast search for artists' own unique voices, which could be attained through the intertwining of Chinese and Surrealist iconography. Surrealism, more than any other modernist movement, could provide a Chinese artist with such a toolkit through its core ideological bedrock of Freudian psychoanalysis, which provided a catalyst for self-reflection and expression. At its height, the Surrealist dreamscape combined individual and collective concerns, being used to manifest political dystopia as we see in the case of photomontage artists and Pang Xunqin, while other artists used notions such as automatism, incongruous juxtaposition, assemblage, appropriation, and the marvellous to dialectically blur the lines between dream and reality in the resoundingly contradictory city of Shanghai where everyday existence was torn between tradition and modernity, colonialism and feudalism.

Shanghai's French Concession formed a geographic locus where all of these different elements came into play, a haven for returnee Chinese students who had studied abroad in both France and Japan to put their training in Western art into practice. In turn, Surrealism, at its core, contains elements of Chinese thought, particularly the Daoist concept of *wuwei* or 'non-action', the movement advocating a revolution of the mind as a means to a revolution in society. Indeed, Girard, a French Surrealist artist and critic, points out that Daoism has been significant in Chinese social history, catalysing many peasant revolts.[1] Moreover, the tension in Surrealism between collective revolution and individual desire is reified by Shanghainese elaborations of the female nude. Lang Jingshan first introduced classical female beauty into Shanghai print culture in 1928 through the genre of photography and its indexical relation to reality before experimenting with Surrealist techniques. Anathema to Chinese artistic tradition, the nude could be – as in Western Surrealist practice – distorted, debased, and dismembered in an expression of rising political tension displaced onto the deeply personal realm of desire as per the predilections of *manhua* artists. A testament to its global appeal, Surrealism is not a culturally specific movement and has been adapted and assimilated in many diverse nations and cultures, from Egypt to Peru and Japan.

Despite its Parisian origins, it is in no way 'French' but a cosmopolitan hybrid, buoyed by the innovations of émigré artists. In turn, Shanghai, carved up into foreign concessions,

1. Guy Girard, 'Taoism', in *The International Encyclopedia of Surrealism* edited by M. Richardson, D. Ades, K. Fijalkowski, S. Harris and G. Sebbag (Bloomsbury Visual Arts: London, 2019): 308–311.

was viewed by many citizens as distinct from being 'Chinese'. Of course, Surrealism was not alone in appealing to Chinese artists, increasingly trained in all forms of modern and realist Western painting. Cubism and its reassembling of fragmented parts, the vivid and non-representational colour palettes of Post-Impressionism and Fauvism along with Dadaism's irrationality all left an indelible mark on Shanghai, despite the fact their zenith of influence had already passed in Europe. These movements were also 'grabbed' in Shanghai at the same time as Surrealism during the 1930s. However, the interdisciplinarity of Surrealism as a movement encompassing literature, poetry, painting, photography, psychoanalysis, and politics arguably enjoyed one of the most widespread presences among the pictorials and periodicals of the era, whether formally acknowledged (as was the case of the Storm Society and CIAA) or otherwise. Moreover, it is perhaps Surrealism that best expresses the idiosyncrasies of Shanghai, an uncanny city where everyday reality was at once resoundingly strange yet familiar. Surrealism was also a highly active movement in the West during the 1930s, and as such, the most modern of all cultural borrowings.

Ultimately, both the European and Chinese Surrealist factions suffered the same fate, dispersal at the onset of the Second Sino-Japanese War in 1937 which merged into what we know in the West as the Second World War from 1939. Shanghai fell to the Japanese early in the conflict in November 1937. While Surrealism appeared sporadically until the end of the Chinese Civil War in 1949, Chinese modernism was largely limited to clandestine underground activities during the Mao era, with only fellow travellers of Communism such as Mexican muralists and Picasso allowed to be shown. Surrealism, however, was thoroughly resurrected after the reform and opening up of China in 1978. With relaxed restrictions on individual expression, the Chinese art world was once again overwhelmed by Western modernist currents from the 1930s, the style of Socialist Realism prescribed by Mao's Communist party perpetuating a timeless heterotopia of idealised reality until that juncture. Surrealism was once again used by contemporary Chinese artists such as Zhang Xiaogang as a means to evoke the traumatic vestiges of the Cultural Revolution in his *Bloodlines* series (1993–present) as well as sentiments of a dreamlike new-found freedom in the case of Meng Luding and Zhang Qun's *The Revelation of Adam and Eve* (1985).

Historically speaking, a plethora of European-based Surrealists clearly drew inspiration from both modern and traditional China. Several European Surrealists were taken with Chinese calligraphy, including Jean Degottex. In 1955, André Breton himself would open his exhibition of calligraphy-inspired paintings. After the Second World War, André Masson began to study Sinology, while Michel Leiris wrote an ethnographic travelogue dedicated to his escapades in China. Salvador Dalí would somewhat inexplicably sketch Chairman Mao.

Despite the lack of recognition of Chinese Surrealists by their European counterparts, it is clear that the nascent presence of Surrealism in China, first fomented during the 1930s, continues to exert an enduring influence on Chinese artists today. Moreover, the cultural hybridity and coalescing of avant-garde Western philosophy with reinvigorated Chinese cultural traditions established Shanghai's French Concession as the centre of the Chinese art world in an early twentieth-century context, so much so that the city became known as the 'Paris of the East'. Hopefully this book has provided a small contribution towards destabilising the orientalist simplification inherent in this terminology, through elaborating the intricacies of Surrealism's reception in Shanghai.

APPENDIX I: THE STORM SOCIETY MANIFESTO (1932)

环绕我们的空气太沉寂了，平凡与庸俗包围了我们的四周。无数低能者的蠢动，无数浅薄者的叫嚣。

我们往古创造的天才到哪里去了？我们往古光荣的历史到哪里去了？我们现代整个的艺术界只是衰颓和病弱。

我们再不能安于这样妥协的环境中。

我们再不能任其奄奄一息以待毙。

让我们起来吧！用了狂飙一般的激情，铁一般的理智，来创造我们色•线•形交错的世界吧！

我们承认绘画决不是自然的模仿，也不是死板的形骸的反覆，我们要用全生命来赤裸裸地表现我们泼剌的精神。

我们以为绘画决不是宗教的奴隶，也不是文学的说明，我们要自由地、综合地构成纯造型的世界。

我们厌恶一切旧的形势，旧的色彩，厌恶一切平凡低级的技巧。 我们要用新的技法来表现新时代的精神。

二十世纪以来，欧洲的艺坛突现新兴的气象，野兽群的叫喊，立体派的变形，Dadaism 的猛烈，超现实主义的憧憬……。

二十世纪的中国艺坛，也应当现出一种新兴的气象了。

让我们起来吧！用了狂飙一般的激情，铁一般的理智，来创造我们色·线·形交错的世界吧！

A stultified air envelops us, a banal vulgarity is all around, innumerable imbeciles go about their ways and superficial crowds clamour.

Where have all our past geniuses gone? Where did our glorious history vanish? Our current art world is synonymous with sickness and decay.

We can no longer tolerate this intellectual climate.

We can no longer ignore the death rattles.

Let's us rise up with burning passion, creating a world of colour, line and form out of iron-clad rationality.

We believe painting is not a product of imitating nature, nor the product of laborious repetition, we must lay bare our own lives to manifest our ferocious spirit.

We believe art is not a slave to religion, nor is it a mere accompaniment to literature, instead, we aim to freely compose an independent universe of shape and colour.

We detest outmoded forms, colours and techniques, we must innovate our practice to usher in the spirit of the new era.

Since the beginning of the 20th century, the European art world has witnessed the advent of new phenomena: the cries of the Fauvists, the deformations of Cubism, the vehemence of Dada and the desires of the Surrealists.

The art world in 20th century China should also foster this new atmosphere.

Let's us rise up with burning passion, creating a world of colour, line and form out of iron-clad rationality.

Yishu Xunkan [Art trimonthly] 1, no. 5 (October 1932): 8.

APPENDIX II: MANIFESTO OF THE CHINESE INDEPENDENT ART ASSOCIATION (1935)

LI DONGPING

美术家之集团的运动是非使各自的艺术自由地发展向上不可，如那样才有社会存在的意义吧！因此，我们对于从来美术团体的运动是极表同情的，但可惜得很，我国艺术界之"时代迟"这又不能不使我们感叹的，法兰西之"独立美术家协会"（La Société des Artistes Independents）已是五十二周年了，回顾我国美术界还是蹒跚着他底崎途；我们为着谋我国美术界急入平坦道路而更欲其一日千里起见，于是我们的"独立美术协会"乃根此而产生了。

我们是以新的绘画精神为基点更为本会之方向，我们需要的是新时代的绘画，……我们专以创作的自由与独立为社会文化之前卫向一般公众去着力，同时，我们立在我们之自信上，不管对我们间的毁誉和褒贬，我们祈愿地前进，我们在远大的理想下执着我们不动的信念和不挠的忍耐而前进。

我们公募作品，开始我们独立美术协会堕地之第一声，震撼全国还向世界去，……把美的主张自由赤裸裸地向着公众之前呼叫，这是我们所期望的，也是我们独立美术协会的使命。

The activities of artist collectives should propel the development of creative freedom in a way that is valued by society. Whilst we are most sympathetic to the efforts of previous groups, it is a shame that the art world in our country is lagging behind, we can't help but sigh. The French [SOCIÉTÉ DES ARTISTES INDEPENDANTS] has already celebrated its fifty-second anniversary. Looking back, our country is still limping along the wrong path. Our independent art association is borne out of the desire to find a newer, smoother road, ensuring rapid progress for the Chinese art world.

The new spirit of painting [L'ESPRIT NOUVEAU] is our foundation and our stylistic direction [ORIENTATION]. We respect all doctrines and viewpoints within this new era and new spirit. Our mission is to create a free and independent social and cultural avant-garde for everyone. At the same time, we stand proudly with the self-confidence that no matter the criticism or praise received, we will advance with hope. With unshakable faith and unwavering patience, we move forward under our lofty ideals.

Presenting our works in public brought us back down to earth with a bang, shocking the whole country, even spreading to the wider world. Crying out the idea of beauty nakedly to the masses, this is the purpose and mission of our independent art association.

Duli Meishu [Independent art] March 1935, inaugural issue.

APPENDIX III: BIOGRAPHIES

Dai Wangshu (1905–1950)
Important Chinese literary figure who studied French at the Université de L'Aurore in Shanghai's French Concession, graduating in 1926. During his time at L'Aurore, he was arrested on suspicion of being a communist but later released. He studied abroad in Lyon between 1932 and 1935 and reported back on events for Shi Zhecun's periodical *Xiandai* [Les Contemporains]. He met Surrealist founder André Breton while in France and asked Shi Zhecun through Surrealist member Eugène Jolas to dedicate a special edition of *Xiandai* on Surrealism, something that never materialised. He fled to Hong Kong during the Second Sino-Japanese War (1937–1945) and was imprisoned by Japanese authorities in 1942. He began to work as an editor and translator for the Chinese Communist Party in 1949 but died a year later of ill health.

Duan Pingyou (1906–?)
Born in Hunan, Duan Pingyou studied at the Shanghai Art College before entering the Storm Society in 1932. He produced Picasso-esque nudes against scenic backdrops.

Fu Lei (1908–1966)
Francophile translator and critic who studied literature and art history between 1928 and 1931 at the University of Paris. He

translated French Surrealist author Phillipe Soupault's 'Chaplin' into Chinese in 1931 and identified Pang Xunqin's works as Surrealist. He was labelled as a rightist in 1957, the ensuing persecution causing he and his wife to take their own lives in 1966. Between 1954 and 1966, he wrote heartfelt letters to his son, who was studying piano in Poland, which are considered an important part of the Chinese cultural memory of that era.

Guo Jianying (1907–1979)
Studied politics and economics at St John's University Shanghai and began his career as a banking secretary in 1931. He also served at the Chinese consulate in Nagasaki, Japan, between 1935 and 1937. These roles were combined with a literary and cartooning career. He was editor of *Funu Huabao* [Women's pictorial] between 1934 and 1935 and produced many erotic renderings of the female form that resonate with Surrealism.

Lang Jingshan (1892–1995)
Dubbed the 'father of Asian photography', Lang began his career in Shanghai as a photojournalist. In 1928, he is considered to have taken the first published fine art photograph of a nude model. His engagement with Surrealism was primarily on a technical basis. He created the method of 'composite photography' where different negatives would be merged together. This would often also be combined with paintings, particularly traditional Chinese landscapes. After the Chinese Civil War (1945–1949), Lang moved to Taiwan and continued his photographic experimentation, this time directly utilising Man Ray's technique of rayography to invert colour. He met Man Ray in Paris in 1960 and 1974. A photograph of Marcel Duchamp is also conserved in his archives.

Lei Guiyuan (1905–1989)
Born in Songjiang, Shanghai. Studied abroad in Paris in 1929 and taught at the Hangzhou Academy in 1931 upon returning to China.

During the Second Sino-Japanese War (1937–1945), he established China's first design school in 1939. After the founding of the People's Republic of China (PRC) in 1949, he taught at the Central Academy of Fine Arts in Beijing. Throughout his career, he published several books on theories of pattern design.

Liang Baibo (1911–1970)
A female cartoonist and artist born into a middle-class background. She participated in the first and fourth Storm Society exhibitions. She was one of only two female members of the Storm Society (the other being Pang Xunqin's wife Qiu Ti). She drew under the pen name 'bon', French for 'good', having been advised to drop her former signature 'bomb' given its turbulent social context. She is famous for her 'Miss Bee' sketches of a bourgeois Shanghai 'modern girl' figure. She frequently sketched in a Surrealist style, potentially as a parody of male voyeurism. During the Second Sino-Japanese War, she was a member of the Shanghai Cartoon Salvation Corps, where she aimed to mobilise female resistance. She also utilised Surrealist techniques such as headlessness to portray the violence of enemy forces. Liang moved to Taiwan after the founding of the PRC where she struggled to gain recognition, suffered from schizophrenia, and ultimately committed suicide.

Pang Xunqin (1906–1985)
Pang Xunqin was born into a middle-class family in Jiangsu province. In 1925, he studied medicine at the French-language Université de L'Aurore in Shanghai's French Concession. Here, a French Jesuit priest told Pang he could never become a great painter due to his Chinese nationality, yet Pang decided to travel to Paris to prove himself. Between 1925 and 1929, Pang lived in Paris and enrolled initially in the Académie Julian, but in 1926, at the suggestion of his friend fellow Chinese painter Sanyu, he changed to the more liberal Académie de la Grande Chaumière. Hoping to find his own artistic voice, Pang moved back to China after four years abroad. New

Sensationist writer Shi Zhecun noted that the works Pang bought back from Paris were 'almost all Surrealist'. In 1932, Pang taught at the Shanghai Art College and became a founding member of the Storm Society, participating in all four of the group's exhibitions until 1935. During the Second Sino-Japanese War, Pang relocated to Kunming and began to work for the Central Museum who sent him to research the folk art of Miao minority peoples. During the Mao era (1949–1976), although Pang's modernism was criticised, he held many teaching roles and concentrated on the decorative arts. In the early 1980s, before his passing, his earlier works were rehabilitated and became a reference point for artists associated with China's '85 New Wave, a second blossoming of the avant-garde.

Sanyu (1895–1966)

Sanyu (Chang Yu) was born into a wealthy family in Sichuan province who owned a silk factory of which his brother Chang Junmin became the manager. Sanyu was trained in traditional painting and calligraphic techniques as a child. Chang Junmin supported his brother's artistic talents and in 1921 Sanyu moved to Paris to pursue his passion studying at the Académie de la Grande Chaumière, specialising in nude drawing. He likely sketched Surrealist muse Kiki de Montparnasse. The spontaneity of his calligraphic stroke and Picasso-inspired drawing style resonates with Surrealist automatism. He attracted the attention of French dealer Henri Pierre Roché who was also representing Picasso. Through Roché, it is likely that Sanyu and Picasso became acquainted. Indeed, in 1945, he published the essay 'Opinions of a Chinese Painter on Picasso'. Despite some commercial success via Roché during the 1930s, Sanyu remained poor throughout this life and died prematurely at his Parisian studio due to a gas leak.

Shi Zhecun (1905–2003)

Important literary figure in Republican China who attended the Université de L'Aurore in Shanghai's French Concession. He was a member of the New Sensationist group who used Freudian psychoanalysis in his short stories. Also editor of the journal *Xiandai* [Les Contemporains], he was approached by Surrealist Eugène Jolas via Chinese author Dai Wangshu, who was based in Paris at the time, to edit a special edition on the Surrealist movement. Shi refused stating that the movement may have been viewed as escapism. Nonetheless, several Surrealist front covers and articles indicating news about Surrealism appeared in this periodical. Shi taught literature in Kunming during the Second Sino-Japanese War. His work was banned during the Mao era as decadent, but he was rehabilitated during the reform and opening up (1978).

Wang Zimei (1913–2002)

Engaged in cartooning in Shanghai between 1935 and 1937. He joined the National Cartoon Salvation Corps during the Second Sino-Japanese War. During the Chinese Civil War he published several works lampooning Nationalist Party leader Chiang Kai-shek, for which he was almost arrested. After the communists gained power, he worked as the vice chairman of the Chongqing Artists Association but was labelled a rightist in 1958. In 1980 he was rehabilitated and became the library director of the Sichuan Academy of Fine Arts.

Yang Taiyang (1909–2009)

Yang was born in Guilin, Guanxi province. He was educated at the Shanghai Art College majoring in Western painting and, after graduating in 1931, joined the Storm Society in 1932. He exhibited paintings featuring the Surrealist technique of incongruous juxtapositions. In 1935, after the final Storm Society exhibition, he studied abroad in Japan. He resided in Hong Kong during the Second Sino-Japanese War, and after the founding of the PRC served in several leadership roles, notably as vice president of the Guangzhou Academy of Fine Art. His oeuvre rapidly changed from Surrealism to watercolour landscapes.

Ye Lingfeng (1905–1975)
A painter and writer who moved to Shanghai in 1924. He entered the Shanghai Academy of Fine Arts and was associated with the New Sensationist school, drawing from Freudian psychoanalysis. He moved to Hong Kong in 1938 to escape the Second Sino-Japanese War where he worked clandestinely for the Nationalist Party. He was caught and imprisoned by the Japanese in 1942. He remained in Hong Kong for the rest of his life.

Zeng Ming (dates unknown)
Zeng Ming's place of birth is unknown. He studied abroad in Japan from 1932 to 1934 and became a founding member of the CIAA. In the *Yifeng* [Art winds] special edition on Surrealism (1935), he is formally identified as a Surrealist alongside Zhao Shou. He continued to publish articles and his works continued to feature in modern art periodicals during 1936 and 1937 but no trace is found of him after the outbreak of the Second Sino-Japanese War.

Zhang Guangyu (1900–1965)
Born in Wuxi, Jiangsu province, Zhang moved to Shanghai in 1918 to study and made advertisements for a tobacco company. He also contributed to *manhua* publications in the city, creating Surrealist front covers for several outlets. He lived in Hong Kong during the Second Sino-Japanese War and in 1945 produced a cartoon version of the Daoist legend *Journey to the West* (The Monkey King) comprising allegorical condemnation of the Nationalist Party. After the founding of the PRC, Zhang worked as head of the Decorative Arts section of the Central Academy of Fine Art in Beijing between 1949 and 1963.

Zhang Xian (1893–1936)
Zhang Xian was part of a wave of artists who studied abroad in France, where he met fellow artist Pang Xunqin. During the early 1920s, he was admitted to the École Nationale Supérieure des

Beaux-Arts where he was taught Western painting. Upon his return to China, he taught at the Shanghai Art College and joined the Storm Society in 1932. His work submitted to the first Storm Society exhibition (1932) exhibited knowledge of surrealistic collage principles. He died prematurely, reportedly in poverty.

Zhao Shou (1912–2003)
Zhao Shao was born in Guangdong province and attended the Guangzhou Municipal Art School, graduating in 1931. In 1933, he studied abroad in Japan where the CIAA was founded. The group held Surrealist exhibitions in Tokyo in 1934 and in Guangzhou and Shanghai in 1935. To accompany the Shanghai exhibition, he translated André Breton's Surrealist Manifesto into Chinese and contributed an imaginative ode to Pablo Picasso in the special edition of *Yifeng* [Art winds] magazine, dedicated to introducing Surrealism. Zhao Shou remained committed to Surrealism throughout his career, including the Maoist era where he found himself 'sent down to the countryside' in 1958 on trumped-up charges, continuing his artistic practice clandestinely. After the reform and opening up (1978), his work gained international recognition and in 1998 two of his pieces featured in the 'China: Five Thousand Years Civilisation' exhibition at the Guggenheim Museum, New York.

Zhou Duo (1905–?)
Member of the Storm Society who had studied abroad in Japan and at the Shanghai Art College. His work submitted to the second Storm Society exhibition (1933) demonstrated knowledge of Surrealist assemblage as did a front cover for *Xiandai* magazine. He moved to Taiwan after the founding of the PRC and ceased painting at that juncture.